# HE
# Speaks
# TO Me

## JILL LOWRY

ISBN-13: 978-1-7371825-4-2

**He Speaks to Me**

Cover & Scripture Images Designed by Kerry Prater.
Interior Design by Katharine E. Hamilton

# DEDICATION

This book is dedicated to my precious granddaughter, Landry Elizabeth. When I look into your beautiful eyes and you smile at me, I see the light and love of Jesus.
Gigi loves you so very much!

# INTRODUCTION

Do you hear the voice of Jesus speaking to you? I have discovered that He speaks to me in the stillness of my soul when I spend time reading His words written in red in my Bible. I am amazed at how much I have heard the voice of Jesus while writing this devotional, "He Speaks to Me."

You will read only the red letter statements of Jesus in this daily devotional. After you read the scripture for the day, read the devotion and pray for Jesus to speak to you. If you have more time each day, open your bible and read the whole chapter where the scripture is located. Meditate on the red letter words of Jesus and then listen to how Jesus will put hope in your heart. He wants to have deeper conversations with you.

Open your heart and get ready for Jesus to speak to you through His red letters. Be still and know that He will share His treasures of truth and promises of hope to set your heart on fire. You will find your joy in Jesus as you pray from your heart and read His love letters to you.

# In the Garden

I come to the garden alone,
While the dew is still on the roses,
And the voice I hear falling on my ear,
The Son of God discloses...

And He walks with me, and He talks with me,
And He tells me I am His own,
And the joy we share as we tarry there,
None other, has ever, known!

He speaks and the sound of His voice,
Is so sweet the birds hush their singing,
And the melody that he gave to me,
Within my heart is ringing . . .

And He walks with me, and He talks with me,
And He tells me I am His own,
And the joy we share as we tarry there,
None other, has ever, known!

And the joy we share as we tarry there,
None other, has ever, known!

Words and Music by C. Austin Miles, 1912
C. Austin Miles, 1868-1946

# Do you believe

## THAT I AM ABLE

## TO DO THIS?

MATTHEW 9:28

# January 1

*"But seek first the kingdom of God and his righteousness, and all these things will be added to you."*
*Matthew 6:33*

We all seek more. But are we seeking more of God or more things? Jesus tells us that when we seek more of God and put Him first, He will add more to our lives. Instead of striving for more earthly things, try seeking more of God through the open door of Jesus Christ.

He will not only enrich your life with heavenly blessings which remain forever, but He will bless you with spiritual blessings in this life on earth. No one can take away His love. There is nothing that can separate you from His eternal love. He has written your name in the palm of His hand.

Who is first in your life? If Jesus is not in first place, pray that you would hear his plea to seek Him above all, so that your life will be sealed with spiritual blessings from above. If He is first, be still and hear Him speaking love to your heart. He will fill your cup and add the sweet taste of honey to your lips. Is your cup full of Jesus or earthly things?

# January 2

*"Be silent, and come out of him!"*
**Mark 1:25**

Jesus will protect us when we are attacked. He knows there is darkness in this world, but He can remove the darkness with just a mere touch of His light. The world's influences are trying to pull us away from Jesus, but He can speak the light into the darkness and drive out any evil lurking in our lives.

He will silence those who try to hurt you. He is your Defender ready to fight for you. He knows what it is like to be tempted and persecuted. He will stand strong for you, when you stand firm for Him. Turn toward the light and step away from the dark. When you let Jesus fight your battle, good will prevail over evil. The victory has already been won.

What battle are you facing today? Has the world tried to convince you there is nothing you can do? Listen to Jesus speaking with authority to the enemy and pray that you will believe He will fight for you. Ask Him for help and step away from sin. He will stand with you when you put His armor on and raise up your sword of the spirit, the Word of God. Raise it high!

# January 3

*"Why do you call me 'Lord, Lord,'*
*and not do what I tell you?"*
*Luke 6:46*

Jesus wants us to not only listen to Him, but also to obey what He tells us because He loves us. When we obey Him, we show our love for Him. He will manifest Himself to us as we live in relationship with Him. He knows everything we will go through even before it happens, and He knows what is best for us.

He came to set you free from the lies you have been told, so open your heart and He will guide you to all truth. He will direct your heart to know the way to go as you let Him love you. He needs you to come closer so He can pour peace over your problems.

What problem has you distracted? Pray for your eyes to see and your ears to hear what Jesus says to do. Envision His arms comforting you because He knows what you need. Let Jesus speak to your heart right now. He has so much to tell you. Listen with love and watch Jesus change you from the inside out, because you are gifted with His grace.

# January 4

*"Truly, truly I say to you, you will see heaven opened, and the angels of God ascending and descending on the Son of Man."*
**John 1:51**

We will see so much when we place our faith in the Savior, Jesus Christ. He has promised His followers they will see heaven opened up one day. We can only imagine what it will be like. But we know that Jesus promises a place unlike anything our brain can comprehend. We will also see angels of God all around the Son of Man. Oh, what a day that will be!

Are you sure of your salvation? Have you made the decision to follow Jesus? He wants you to make this most important decision of your life. When you do, you will have all these promises because, you will be a child of God. He wants you to follow Him.

Do not wait another day. Heaven is real and will be your forever home if you believe and give Jesus your heart. Pray for faith from Jesus to believe in Him. Your faith will be your eyes and joy will flood your heart with Jesus by your side. Run to the One who loves you!

# January 5

*"Temptations to sin are sure to come, but woe to the one through whom they come!"*
**Luke 17:1**

We will all be tempted at some point. But we can remain faithful if we place our trust in Jesus, listen to the voice of the Holy Spirit showing us what is right, and then do it. The flesh is weak, so the Spirit of God has been given to us to help us in our times of weakness. There is great hope knowing that we can conquer every temptation if we call out to Jesus for help, even before we know we need Him.

What are you trying to hide from God? Remember, He sees and knows every thought you have. Jesus wants to help you stay away from sin, for He knows the woe that will come to those who make the choice to listen to the flesh and not the spirit. He wants to set you free and see you healed.

Pray for God to give you a way out when the temptation comes. He always provides a path of light where you can escape the darkness. Even in a total eclipse of the sun, Jesus, His Son is not eclipsed, for His light shines the brightest in the dark. Draw to the light of the world, Jesus Christ!

# January 6

*"And if any place will not receive you and they will not listen to you, when you leave, shake off the dust that is on your feet as a testimony against them."*
*Mark 6:11*

Jesus wants us to reach people. He needs us to be His hands and feet on the earth. But He also knows there are some who will not receive His message. If you cannot reach them, leave knowing they need Jesus. Pray they will find the way to peace through Jesus Christ soon.

Who has rejected you when you reached out? Pray for them. Believe they will eventually come to Jesus, because He lives to save the lost. He loves even those who reject Him. Shake off the negativity and resistance from these people. Your witness is commanded by Jesus even if they turn their backs and do not listen to you. He wants all to be saved.

What can you do? Keep speaking truth to build the kingdom of God. Give your time so the love of Jesus can be seen through you. Be kind so others will know they are loved. Make every effort to love with a pure heart, a good conscience, and a sincere faith, and you will be blessed, indeed. Whatever you do, always do it for the glory of God!

# January 7

*"Blessed are the poor in spirit, for theirs is the*
*kingdom of heaven."*
**Matthew 5:3**

Jesus gives us blessings to hold onto even when we are troubled and heavily burdened. He brings people into our lives at just the right time who speak exactly what we need to hear when we are doubting ourselves. He places us in situations where we feel unworthy, but He knows if we stay there, we will be right where He needs us to grow our faith. We grow closer to Jesus in the most challenging times.

Whatever challenges you are facing, know that Jesus has experienced even more. He has more grace for you than you deserve and more love than you can wrap your mind around. If your spirit is weak, you need more of Jesus. His kingdom is full of love, joy, peace, patience, kindness, goodness, faithfulness, gentleness and self-control.

Where are you struggling with right now? Instead of isolating yourself, Jesus wants to lead you. If you feel like your world is falling apart, Jesus wants you to know He will bless you with the keys to the kingdom. His kingdom is centered on love and grace. Everyone is welcome, especially those who are poor in spirit!

HE SPEAKS TO ME

# *January 8*

*"The kingdom of heaven is like treasure hidden in a
field, which a man found and covered up. Then in
his joy he goes and sells all that he has and buys
that field."*
*Matthew 13:44*

Jesus fills us with the desire to seek treasures from
heaven when we are close to Him. He gives us
glimpses of heaven when we grow spiritually.
Our hearts will bloom with joy when we let Jesus be
our strength and our song. The kingdom is alive in us
as followers of Jesus.

Are you following Jesus? He wants to show you great
and mighty things for His glory. He has hand-picked
you to follow Him so He can show you more. Joy will
come to you if you let His love grow bountifully in
your heart and soul. Make room for Jesus so the
kingdom of heaven will be your forever home.

Where do you need growth? Jesus will grow a
garden of love in the good soil of your heart. Pray He
will show you where you need to open more of
yourself to Him and then surrender that part to the
Lord so His roots will grow deeper in you. He will
bring your soul the overflowing joy you have been
searching for.

# January 9

*"It is written, "'You shall worship the Lord your God, and him only shall you serve.'"*
**Luke 4:8**

Jesus was tempted and did not waiver in His strength. He remained close to God, trusted Him, and stood firm on His Word. He knew that we, too, would be enticed by worldly things, so He has given us the Word so we can rely on His promises no matter what comes our way. Remember what is written and worship the Lord God so He will be close when the problems come.

Have you praised the Lord today? Thank Him for all He has done and let His love enrich your heart. The more you worship Him, the more He will come alive in you. He will revive you as you let the Holy Spirit breathe on you. Pray for a fresh filling of the Spirit in your life and watch Him work His miracles in you.

Open your heart to worship and serve the Lord and find the blessings that will come to you. It is more blessed to give than receive. God knows you will be able to stand as you stay connected to Him. Think of ways you can serve and step out. Someone is waiting for you!

# January 10

*"I told you, and you do not believe. The works that I do in my Father's name bear witness about me."*
*John 10:25*

Jesus speaks about the works He does in His Father's name that bear witness about Him. These works point us to believe. Jesus wants us to know He and the Father are one and that they love us. When we put faith first, works will follow.

Do you have faith? If Jesus is your Lord, His grace will activate the faith needed to grow a closer relationship with Him. And when you have this relationship with Jesus, you will know the Father's love as well. They will come to you and make their home with you.

If you want to be content, set your hope on the living God. He gives you many reasons to trust Him beginning with His grace and ending with His promise of eternal life. Remember, Jesus will give you the faith you need to do the works He wants you to do. Will you make the choice to work with Jesus so He can do His kingdom work in you?

# January 11

*"I have said all these things to you to keep you from falling away."*
*John 16:1*

Jesus helps us stay on the right path so we do not fall away. He guides us so that we do not give up before He can show us the way to go. Only Jesus knows just when we need a little push to go the extra mile. He is the one who gives us more strength to conquer our fears. So, trust Jesus every step of the way.

Jesus wants the best for you, so keep pressing on with Him and He will take you through whatever you are going through. He knows your fears and sees your tears, dear one. Trust Him to take you where you need to go and watch Him show you how to live from victory and not defeat.

Where do you need to see some encouragement? Start focusing on what Jesus can do and ask Him to bring it to you. Fall toward Jesus instead of away from Him. Positivity begets praise and gratitude, so begin each day thanking God for all your blessings instead of worrying about your problems. Live an abundant life with Jesus by your side and in your heart!

# *January 12*

*"When you are invited by someone to a wedding feast, do not sit down in a place of honor, lest someone more distinguished than you be invited by him."*
*Luke 14:8*

Jesus sees us and loves us. He says that we are distinguished in His eyes because we are His children. In His kingdom, the last are the first and the first are the last. Jesus knows where we belong and to whose we belong to and invites all to His table of grace. Come to the table where all are welcome.

Are you afraid of not being included or have a fear of missing out? Watch and wait for Jesus to let you in. He has invited you. There is room for you where Jesus is seated. He calls you worthy and wanted no matter how other people treat you.

Pray that you will make every effort to love gently and gracefully. Jesus has a special place for you, so let others go before you and put their interests above yours and He will bountifully bless your heart and soul. He has included you so you can invite others who need to know Jesus as their Lord and Savior.

# January 13

*"All authority in heaven and on earth
has been given to me."*
*Matthew 28:18*

Jesus has reminded us that He has all authority in
heaven and Earth. His powerful presence is
always with us. He will show us His love that
remains when we are still in His presence. He will
seal us with the Holy Spirit as we believe. Remember
His promises and stay closely connected to Him.

Are you looking for love and need confirmation of
the love Jesus has just for you? Recognize His voice
calling you and let Him lead you closer to Him. He
has authority over you with His plans for good, and
not for harm, to give you a future and a hope.

The heavens are calling out to you to give Jesus your
whole heart. He is looking far and wide to find those
who are faithful. Are you one of the faithful few? If
so, let Him know by living out your faith right now.
He is looking for you!

# January 14

*"With what can we compare the kingdom of God, or
what parable shall we use for it?"*
**Mark 4:30**

The kingdom of God is home for us who believe. God is amazing and His kingdom is greater than anything we can ever imagine. How can we describe such a wonderful love that we have as a child of the living God? His love is real and available for all of us to receive with hearts wide open.

Have you thought about how much God loves you that He gave His only begotten Son so that you will not perish but have everlasting life? If not for Jesus, you would not have forgiveness of your sins or know the unconditional love of the Father. Now, that is amazing grace!

Jesus wants you to think about how special it is to be a part of the family of God. His family is united with one mind, one heart, and one spirit. Nothing can compare to the glory that you will experience when you are resurrected and receive your heavenly body. You are now one of His because you chose to be counted as saved!

# *January 15*

*"Go into all the world and proclaim the gospel to the whole creation."*
*Mark 16:15*

We are commanded by Jesus to go into the world and share the gospel. We are to proclaim it to all creation. We are also commanded to be a witness to all by testifying as to what Jesus has done in our lives. We are to live boldly with great faith for all the world to see.

Who needs to hear your testimony of what Jesus has done for you? Who needs to know that Jesus has not given up on them, but loves them with an everlasting love? Spread the message of the love of Jesus and His sweet aroma will permeate the place where you proclaim His precious love.

Jesus loves the whole world. He wants to save the lost. He needs you to be His hands and feet so you can bring good news of great joy to all the people you see. What are you waiting for? Come now and bring His hope to this broken and lost world who needs a Savior like yours!

# January 16

*"I tell you, he will give justice to them speedily.
Nevertheless, when the Son of Man comes, will he
find faith on earth?"*
**Luke 18:8**

Jesus proclaims justice. He lifts us up so that we will not be downcast but will rise with wings like eagles. We will run and not be weary and walk and not faint. He is looking for those who have faith to run with Him. He will bring justice to all who need it.

Do you need to be lifted up because your burdens are too heavy? Jesus has given you His promise to be your refuge and strength and a very present help in trouble. He will catch you when you fall and help you overcome your battle. The war is not against flesh and blood, so fight with Jesus by your side.

Make room for Jesus to be your Rock. His justice prevails speedily and surely will come to those who wait upon the Lord. Listen to His gentle spirit urging you to let go and not take revenge yourself. He will bring vengeance to those who hurt your heart. Will the Son of Man find you faithful to Him when He comes?

# January 17

*"I have spoken openly to the world. I have always taught in synagogues and in the temple, where all Jews come together. I have said nothing in secret."*
*John 18:20*

Jesus does not hide His thoughts, but speaks openly to the world. He speaks the truth with boldness so we can know Him personally. He teaches us and leads by example so we can see the light. He knows not all will agree with what He speaks, but He prays for us to believe that He is the Savior of the world.

Did you know that Jesus is praying for you? He yearns for you to come to Him for all that you need. In this world you will have trouble, but take heart, because Jesus has overcome the world. He is greater than any problem you will ever face.

Sweet Jesus loves you as His friend. He cares about what happens to you in your life. He wishes that you would not doubt, but put your faith and trust in Him, the Author of your life and Perfecter of your faith. Speak to Jesus with no more doubts in your mind and He will set you free once and for all!

# January 18

*"I am the true vine,*
*and my Father is the vinedresser."*
*John 15:1*

Apart from Jesus, we can do nothing. He gives us new growth when we stay connected to the vine. We can gain spiritual power when we cling to the life-giving power of Jesus Christ made possible by the Father who perfected the vine for us.

Are you living with the Spirit as power through Jesus? He will bless your life with new health when you drink from His living water. With His water, you will never be dry because He satisfies your every thirst from the life in His branches of the vine. Taste and see that the Lord is good. He is your true vine!

Is your life dry right now? Jesus wants to quench your thirst with His water. You can have all the living water you desire as His well never dries up or leaves you empty. Come to Jesus just as you are, and He will fill your cup until it overflows with great joy. Cling tightly to the vine!

# *January 19*

*"I have earnestly desired to eat this Passover with
you before I suffer."*
**Luke 22:15**

Jesus wants to share a meal with us. He yearns to
have fellowship with each of us. His heart is to
fill ours with exceeding joy. He desires to spend
eternity with us, so He made the ultimate sacrifice by
becoming our Passover lamb. He lives so that we may
live.

Is Jesus Lord of your life? He is calling you into
sweet fellowship with Him so you can experience the
fullness of joy right now and the promise of eternal
life with Him. Take a moment and reflect on what
Jesus has done for you. Thank Him for taking the cup
of suffering so that you can experience life
everlasting.

Do you see how much Jesus loves you? His love
cannot be measured. It flows freely to all who will
receive His blessings. Make Jesus Lord of your life
and discover how much He loves you. There is no
greater love than this: He has laid down His life for
yours. Will you trust Him once and for all?

# January 20

*"Why do you see the speck that is in*

*your brother's eye, but do not notice*
*the log that is in your own eye?"*
*Matthew 7:3*

Jesus sees how we have accused others of wrongdoing but have not taken responsibility for our own actions. It is easier to blame others rather than recognize our own faults. But Jesus wants us to stop judging others and turn toward Him with a repentant heart.

Do you realize that there have been times when you have blamed others for wrongdoing, and you have not recognized your own shortcomings? It is easy to place blame with blind eyes to your own actions. But with Jesus, you can let go of judgment once and for all, because He forgives all.

Pray to see what Jesus is speaking to you about your life, then walk with integrity. Count it all joy when you encounter trials of any kind because it is an opportunity to depend more on Jesus. He will grow your faith and your perseverance even in the hardest of times.

# January 21

*"Do you believe that I am able to do this?"*
*Matthew 9:28*

We are running on empty if we lack faith. And without faith, it is impossible to please God. Jesus reminds us that if we believe, we will see His miracles. He is waiting for us to show Him our faith. Even with the smallest amount of faith, we will see things we have hoped for because with Christ all things are possible.

Jesus loves to see you put your faith in Him. He rewards those who trust Him and live according to His will. Do you believe Jesus is able to do what you are praying for? Have you asked Him for what is in your heart believing that He can do it? Ask in the name of Jesus so He can revive your faith to receive His blessings.

Hope for what you do not yet see and believe all things are possible with God. Keep your faith alive and do not let what others say lead you astray. Listen to the Holy Spirit leading you to the miracle you are seeking. He will surely do it!

# January 22

*"For this statement you may go your way; the*
*demon has left your daughter."*
*Mark 7:29*

J esus listens as we cry out to Him. He hears our
call for help and knows who is attacking us. He
wants to save us from our enemies and will
elevate us to a place of refuge as we call out to Him.
The enemy will leave us alone when we praise God
with our mouths and our hearts.

Are you speaking from fear about what might happen
or from faith about what God can do? Let your faith
rise over fear and God will reign in your life. There is
nothing that is too hard for Him, so trust Him to
defend you when the battle comes your way.

Do you feel under attack? Speak Jesus over the
situation and He will empower you with His strength
to overcome. Remember Jesus will fight your battle,
you only have to be silent. He speaks life over death
and joy over pain.

# January 23

*"No one after lighting a lamp covers it with a jar or puts it under a bed, but puts it on a stand, so that those who enter may see the light."*
*Luke 8:16*

We can share the light by bringing Jesus with us wherever we go. For those who share His truth, the light shines brightly. For those who keep the light of Christ hidden, others around them will remain in darkness. Why are we afraid to shine?

The light of Christ will be seen by all those who enter His presence. Are you shining His light brightly? Shine and let others see Christ in you. People need to see the light, so shine the light from Jesus wherever you go.

Jesus shines the brightest in the darkness. He will not give up lighting up the lives of those who need more of Him. He knows who needs to be ignited and He will use you to spread the flame of His Holy Fire. Will you add a spark of faith to the fire?

# *January 24*

*"I will be with you a little longer, and then I am
going to see him who sent me."*
*John 7:33*

God sent us His Son to love and lavish grace
upon us by His sacrifice. We can have
fellowship with God through Jesus Christ. He
blesses us when we make a choice to spend time with
Him. Jesus came so that we could know the love of
the Father and enter into a relationship with Him.

Have you made the choice to be saved by grace?
Jesus paid it all so that you could have the salvation
you seek and the peace you desire. He wants to get to
know you and loves to share His heart with you. Are
you ready to receive His blessings?

Jesus will show you how He makes all things new.
Beauty arises from ashes and joy replaces weeping
with Jesus in the center of your heart. When He is
your Lord, He will reign over you. Make Jesus a
priority and He will revive you again!

# January 25

*"If you had faith like a grain of mustard seed, you could say to this mulberry tree, 'Be uprooted and planted in the sea,' and it would obey you."*
*Luke 17:6*

Faith is confidence in what we hope for and certainty about what we do not see. Small amounts of faith can grow in our lives to give us great faith when Jesus is the author of our lives. He perfects faith in us when He is our Lord.

Do you have faith even when times are tough, and you cannot understand what is happening? Jesus wants you to trust Him with all your heart and not lean on your own understanding so He can grow your faith. Believe and then trust Him to give you great faith.

When your faith is in Jesus you will experience more. He promises good to those who put their faith, not in other things or people, but in Him alone. Mountain-moving faith will come as you trust Him completely, even when your eyes cannot see. Live by faith, not by sight, so you can believe!

# January 26

*"Let us go across to the other side."*
**Mark 4:35**

The other side looks hard. Leaving our comfort zone can bring fear into our lives. But with Jesus, we are more than conquerors. With Jesus by our side, we can step out with confidence and security no matter what we face.

Are you stepping out of your comfortable place to the other side? Remember Jesus is with you wherever you go. He will guard your heart and strengthen the weak places that keep you from moving closer. The victory is yours in Jesus Christ.

Come all you who are weary and He will bring you rest for your soul and power to go the extra mile. The days are passing quickly, and Jesus wants you to make the most of your time which may include crossing into deep waters. There you will find Jesus waiting for you so He can help you go across to the other side!

# January 27

*"And behold, I am with you always,*
*to the end of the age."*
*Matthew 28:20*

J esus is with us always. He is always close to us and will love us even when we make mistakes. When things seem to be falling apart, Jesus shows us He is putting everything back together again. Fight the good fight of the faith and finish strong.

Do you need to know that Jesus is always with you? He sees the storm you are facing now, what you will encounter soon, and even what you have already been through. He has been with you in every moment and will be with you in the days to come.

Listen to Jesus telling you that He is with you always, even to the end of the age. He wants to encourage you to stay close and let not your heart be troubled or afraid. He sees the beginning and the end. He knows what you are going through now and what you will face in the future. But take heart, and you will rise victoriously with Him!

# January 28

*"But it is easier for heaven and earth to pass away
than for one dot of the Law to become void."*
**Luke 16:17**

God has given us the Law for our good and
wants us to obey the commands to show Him
how much we love Him. We need to keep
listening to God and learning how to write the Word
in our hearts and our minds. When we trust and obey
Jesus, the Way, the Truth and the Life, He and the
Father will be present with us always.

Where can you trust God more? He knows how much
you need His guidance and encouragement. He has
given you Jesus who will live in you so that you can
have an intimate relationship with Him and the Father
of grace. Come to the Father and have all you need
through Jesus Christ.

An explosion of life will come to you when you
follow Jesus. He is calling you to let go and let Him
lead you as you fully surrender. Come just as you are
and bring all your burdens to the fountain of life for a
refreshment of your soul. He is waiting for you with
His open arms of grace.

# January 29

*"Take away the stone."*
**John 11:39**

Nothing is impossible for Jesus. He can do more than we can ever think or imagine when we believe. He showed us that He can heal and bring the dead back to life all for the glory of God. Make the choice to believe and you will see too!

Will you bring Jesus to the impossibilities you are facing? With Him, a miraculous awakening will happen in you if you make the decision to follow Him. Take the first step of faith and roll away the stone that is preventing you from seeing the Truth.

When the stone is removed, the glory will be revealed. Jesus promises life even in the face of death. He will show you where you can trust more to believe again. One simple act of faith can move mountains. Will you move the stone so that you can see?

# January 30

*"And you will be blessed, because they cannot repay you. For you will be repaid at the resurrection of the just."*
**Luke 14:14**

Jesus has given all of us an invitation to His heavenly banquet. He wants us to tell everyone about His saving grace when we work in His kingdom. Not all will believe, but their decision is not up to us. We are called to invite them to know Jesus by bringing His light to them.

Who can you tell about Jesus? Pray that He will bring those people to your heart and mind so that you can invite them to make Jesus Lord of their life. Then go in the highways and hedges and testify about the love and grace of your Savior where He calls you.

With His direction, you will find those who have never been told or who have rejected the invitation before. When a sinner returns to the Lord, He will save them and bless the one who brings them back. Where can you be the hands and feet of Jesus? Many are lost and need to be found, so find them!

# January 31

*"Again it is written, "You shall not put the Lord your God to the test."*
**Matthew 4:7**

When we are unsure about what to do, we need to look at what is written for us to follow in the Word of life. God has given us instructions to obey and promises to cling to in this life and in the eternal life to come. He wants us to read His truth because He loves us and cares deeply for us.

The commandments are given for your good. They are breathed out by the Spirit of God so that you will seek God first. One commandment was spoken by Jesus when He was tempted in the desert. He said that it is written that you shall not put the Lord your God to the test. Are you following this commandment?

He rewards you when you seek Him first. He blesses those that follow faithfully without questioning God. Pray that you will be obedient to listen and trust even when you do not understand. Remember, God knows all and desires to bless your life with heavenly treasures.

YOU SHALL LOVE
*the Lord*
YOUR GOD
*with all your*
HEART,
and with all your soul,
*and with all your*
MIND.

MATTHEW 22:37

# February 1

*"And he said to him, 'Well done, good servant! Because you have been faithful in a very little, you shall have authority over ten cities.'"*
*Luke 19:17*

Our Lord wants us to stay connected to Him. He speaks truth over us so that we know the right way to go. He will never forsake us but will give us opportunities to be faithful when we surrender ourselves to Him and open our hearts to His love.

Have you been listening to Jesus, or have the lies of the world been crowding out the Voice of Truth? Only Jesus can give you the answer to the questions you are asking. He will keep you on the straight and narrow road with Him. The way is hard and those who follow it are few, but with Jesus you can stand firm and faithful.

Jesus will guide you to all truth and give you courage. Call upon Him and let Jesus answer your prayers. He is only a prayer away from you. Keep focused, so you can hear the call of the Lord. Be one of His faithful few by staying the course with Him.

# February 2

*"I who speak to you am he."*
**John 4:26**

Jesus speaks with authority and wants us to know who He is. He is our Messiah who has come to seek and save us. He knows our hearts and hears our every thought. He is also listening when we pray and will let us know how to proceed. We need to have ears to hear what He speaks into our hearts and our minds.

Do you need to hear Jesus? Sit at His feet and let Him teach you all things. He has come to bring light to the situation you are facing right now. He knows how it will all work out and is anticipating your next bold move into the future. He is with you!

Listen, and say yes to the Lord so He can brighten your life again. The light has dimmed in your heart because you are focusing on the wrong things. You can come alive with a fresh filling of the Holy Spirit, dear one. Fix your gaze on the King, and let Him be the king of your heart once and for all!

# February 3

*"You are the salt of the earth, but if salt has lost its taste, how shall its saltiness be restored? It is no longer good for anything except to be thrown out and trampled under people's feet."*
*Matthew 5:13*

We are called to be the salt of the earth to people in word and in deed. We can bring healing or cursing by our mouths. Jesus wants us to bless and not to blame. He desires for us to lift others up, not tear them down. Our actions can bring hope to a hurting world.

How can you help others where Jesus has placed you? Is there someone who needs the love of a Savior? Continue looking at other's interests before yours and encourage them like you are already doing. Jesus sees your actions of love and sacrifice and is well pleased with you.

Can Jesus count on you to make a difference for His kingdom? He is ready to give you another kingdom adventure if you say yes. Do not let your saltiness lose its taste. Restoration is coming and Jesus wants to use you in tremendous ways, faithful one!

# *February 4*

*"I do not say to you seven times,*
*but seventy-seven times."*
*Matthew 18:22*

How often are we to forgive? Jesus tells us that we are to forgive, not seven times, but seventy-seven times. When we do forgive, Jesus forgives us. Our hearts open up in tremendous ways when we let go and forgive those who have wronged us.

Who do you need to forgive? Pray for those people who have hurt you and forgive them. If you hold onto unforgiveness, it will cause bitterness to rise up in your heart. Without forgiveness, you will stay offended, and the Holy Spirit will be quenched in you. Forgive, and you will be forgiven.

Do you need more grace? Ask Jesus who gives graciously to all who ask. His grace is enough and will save you from your sins and give you the desire to forgive again and again. He wipes the slate clean for you when you forgive and receive His amazing grace!

# *February 5*

*"Peace! Be still!"*
**Mark 4:39**

Jesus gives us peace. He knows that we will face uncertainty in this world, so He brings peace to all of us. When tribulations set in, we can call upon the Prince of Peace who brings calm to our lives. Peace is not the absence of trouble, but the presence of Christ.

Are you needing more peace in your life? Be still in His presence and let His peace rule in your heart. Jesus calms the storm when you let Him. He opens the floodgates of peace when you give Him your whole heart and invite Him to rule in your life.

Only Jesus can bring perfect peace to you. Rest with Him and let His presence wipe away every tear and every fear. You have been burdened by many things. He knows what you need and will give it to you freely when you seek Him. Seek the Lord and live!

# *February 6*

*"You shall love the Lord your God with all your heart and with all your soul and with all your mind."*
*Matthew 22:37*

The first and greatest commandment for us to obey is that we are to love the Lord with all our heart, soul, and mind. The Lord loves to see our love for Him. He looks for those who are loving Him so that He can manifest Himself to them in wonderful ways.

You can show God how much you love Him when you become a living sacrifice and stay on His altar of love. If you listen to Him, the Lord will tell you how to stay closely connected. Are you conforming to the what the world says or to what Jesus says?

Keep listening for the Lord. He has something special to say to you. He sees you getting off the altar to live in your flesh again. He wants you to get back up so that He can show you the way to a spirit-filled life full of joy. There is joy in Jesus!

# February 7

*"Father, glorify your name."*
**John 12:28**

The name of the Father brings glory to all. Speak His name to the situation. We need not be afraid to let His power transform us. He will change us, if we let Him come alive in our hearts and give Him praise for all He is doing in and through us.

Where is the Father calling you to grow? Pray that He will show you the places you need to stretch your faith. He has put His Spirit within you so that you will thrive and grow deep roots in Him. His love will come to life in you as your faith deepens in the soil of His love.

Open your mouth, and He will fill it with praise and positivity. He shines brighter in you as you give Him more of your heart and show Him how much you really do love Him. He loves you so much. Where will you shine for God's glory?

# February 8

*"The harvest is plentiful,*
*but the laborers are few."*
Matthew 9:37

The Lord needs us to work for His kingdom to share the gospel with those ready to receive Him. The fields are ripe for harvesting. If we will come and co-labor with Him, He will grow the good fruit for His Kingdom in us for us to share with those who need Jesus.

Who do you know that needs Jesus? Be a bolder witness for His glory to shine through you. Jesus will lift you up to say the words He needs you to share. He will bring those who need Him in your path. Believe there is good in the world and be the good by helping those who are searching for love around you.

How will you show up for Jesus today? Ask Him where he needs you and make every effort to give brotherly love and grace. There are needs you can meet. There are places you can go. His light will shine through you if you commit to being one of His laborers right now!

# February 9

*"Why are you so afraid?*
*Have you still no faith?"*
**Mark 4:40**

Jesus wants to know why we are still afraid. He has placed His Spirit within us to grow our faith. He has given us courage so that we can move forward. He conquered death for us when He sacrificed all so that we can live and have a relationship with Him.

Why are you still so afraid? Remember the price Jesus paid to set you free from fear. Let your faith rise over fear and draw nearer to His voice calling you His beloved. Take His hand and go with Him where He leads you.

That problem you are facing is not too big for Jesus! Pray that you will give it to Him and stop worrying. He will work it out for your good because you love Him and are listening to His voice calling you closer. Have faith over fear, dear child. Jesus loves you!

# *February 10*

*"Truly, I tell you, this poor widow has put in more
than all of them."*
*Luke 21:3*

Jesus sees our efforts and rewards those who give
from their heart without obligation and with
sincerity. He loves to watch us give without
expecting anything in return. Those who give
generously because they want to, and not because
they must, are viewed in the most favorable light.

Have you prayed about where you can give of your
time, talents, and treasures? Jesus is searching for
those who will put service over self. He needs you to
be one of those people. Keep your eyes wide open to
see the needs before and give from your heart like the
poor widow that Jesus encountered.

You will be blessed not by what you get, but by what
you give. Those who give bountifully out of the
abundance of their heart will reap bountifully. See the
needs around you and go meet them. There, you too,
will encounter Jesus Himself!

# *February 11*

*"What I am doing you do not understand now, but
afterward you will understand."*
*John 13:7*

We may not understand why certain things
are happening to us. We might even be
confused as to why we cannot see a way
out of our problems. But nothing is too
big for Jesus to handle. He will lift us up just at the
right time, in the right way.

Are you looking for your own way or Jesus's way?
Direct your way to Jesus by trusting Him with all
your heart and do not lean on your own
understanding. In all your ways acknowledge Him,
and He will make your path straight.

Remember He is the Way. Let Him take the wheel so
He can propel you to your destiny. With Him, you
can navigate the traffic because Jesus will be your
cruise control. Stay on the road with Jesus so He can
get you home!

# *February 12*

*"Take up your bed, and walk."*
**John 5:11**

We all need healing and hope. With Jesus present with us, we can walk confidently and securely because He is our strong tower and place of rest. He is our refuge from life's storms. We can be sure He will provide all we need when we ask in faith.

Do you need healing? Ask in the name of Jesus believing that you shall receive the healing. Take up your bed of pain and sorrow knowing that He is your Healer and Helper who will help you walk again. Jesus wants to see you well and whole.

Pray for God's strength, so you can soar with wings like eagles. Feel His power lift you up and settle your mind. He will satisfy your soul with His infusion of life and give you new energy to handle all the issues you will ever face. You are stronger with Jesus in your heart and soul.

# *February 13*

*Let the little children come to me,*
*and do not hinder them,*
*for to such belongs the kingdom of God."*
*Luke 18:16*

Jesus loves the little children. He has a special love for children who are close to Him, for they belong to the kingdom of God. He sees how we treat these littles ones and pays close attention to our actions toward them. When we love one of His own, we are obeying His command to love.

Do you know a child who needs your time and attention? These little children are all around you waiting to be seen and loved. They may not know how to ask, but you know how to give. Love them so they can see Jesus in you.

Take time today and pray for all of God's little ones to come to Him. Where is God calling you to give your love? God will open your heart to serve as you open yours to love. Make someone smile today.

# February 14

*"Truly, I say to you,*
*today you will be with me in Paradise."*
**Luke 23:43**

Jesus wants all of us to be with Him in Paradise. The thief on the cross next to Jesus believed and was granted entrance into the His kingdom. All of us can make heaven our home when we trust Jesus as our Savior.

Do you need to confess with your mouth that Jesus is your Lord and believe in your heart that He died and rose again so you can be saved? Repent and believe, for He is near to those who call on Him in truth. Call upon His name and ask Him to live forever in your heart and you will be one of His, now and eternally.

Jesus loves and Jesus saves. He has come to take away your sins so you can have a place in His heavenly mansion where there is room for you. Will you hear His call and receive your place in His heart? Make His heart your home.

# *February 15*

*"Unbind him, and let him go."*
*John 11:44*

J esus speaks life into people and situations. He brings hope where doubt exists and peace where pain presides. He raises people to life with the power that lives in Him. There is wonder-working power in the name of Jesus.

Where do you need unbinding so that you can be set free? Jesus is ready to give you new life through His resurrection power. He has softened the hearts of those who have been saved. He has put a heart of flesh in them and taken away their heart of stone. Only Jesus can truly change hearts.

Come to the fountain of life through Jesus Christ. Take His hand and He will refresh your soul. He is offering you His cup that will never run dry. Taste and see that the Lord is good. He will provide the escape and the refuge you are seeking.

# February 16

*"Woman, why are you weeping?*
*Whom are you seeking?"*
*John 20:15*

Jesus sees our tears. He has put them in His bottle and counts each one. He weeps with us and for us. He knows how we are hurting because He feels the emotions we feel. Never fear that Jesus does not see our pain. He does and will comfort us.

Jesus knows the world has chaos that you cannot understand. He knows you feel alone at times because your heart is aching and anxious. But Jesus will come to you just in time. He has overcome the world so that you can have peace.

Have you cried out to Jesus for His help? He will answer your pleas and fulfill your need for peace again. He knows you need Him. Seek Him and you will find Him. He wipes away every tear and brings perfect peace, because He is the Lord Almighty!

# *February 17*

*"According to your faith be it done to you."*
*Matthew 9:29*

J esus loves to see our faith. He rewards those who remain faithful, especially when life gets extremely difficult. When things seem to be falling apart, Jesus comes and puts it all back together in ways even better than we can ever dream or imagine.

Jesus grows your faith as you draw closer to Him. Read His promises to you in the love letters of the Bible. Then pray that you will believe without seeing, and that you will have confidence in what you hope for because you let Jesus reign in you.

What is your hardest problem right now? Believe that Jesus can see you through it and walk with fresh faith. When life brings you a mountain of problems, turn on the mountain-moving faith and see the mountains move!

# February 18

*"For I tell you, you will not see me again, until you say, 'Blessed is he who comes in the name of the Lord.'"*
*Matthew 23:39*

Jesus says He will not see us again until we see Him coming in all His glory. Those who are His will keep praising Him until He comes again. And when He does— Oh what a day that will be! Be encouraged to know that we will be blessed because He will come in the name of the Lord to show us His glory!

Where do you see Jesus moving in your life? He is ever-present in your life when He is Lord of your life. You will be blessed when you praise Him continually with your mouth and believe in your heart that He is Lord.

There are still places for you to go and people for you to see before that marvelous day when He returns in all His glory. He needs you to be a witness to all, so they experience His love. Pray for wisdom about where He needs you to shine.

# *February 19*

*"I have compassion on the crowd, because they have been with me now three days and have nothing to eat."*
*Mark 8:2*

J esus has compassion on all of us. He wants us to feed on His food and drink of His water that gives us life. He knows we all need to be filled, so He gives generously, exactly what we need when we need it.

What are you hungry for? Let Jesus fill you up with His food that satisfies. His food will give you energy to go the extra mile and strength to finish the race. Keep running with endurance because with Jesus you will never run out of fuel.

What are you thirsty for? Let Jesus fill your cup to overflowing with His living water. His water will quench your thirst with springs of water that will never dry up. He will teach you all things that will build your faith.

# *February 20*

*"Look at the birds of the air: they neither sow nor reap nor gather into barns, and yet your heavenly Father feeds them. Are you not of more value than they?"*
*Matthew 6:26*

Why do we worry so much? Our heavenly Father values us and will meet our needs. He wants us to ask and wait patiently on Him to provide. He is there for us all the time. Trust His plan and take His hand.

Do you need to worry less and trust more? Next time you are worried, look at the birds of the air and how they are fed by your Father. You are of more value than the birds. He will provide for you, dear child. Next time you find yourself worrying, speak the name of Jesus over and over and all your anxiety will slowly fade away.

Turn that worry list into a prayer list. Be detailed in your requests. Ask and you shall receive that your joy may be full. You are loved and counted as special in the Father's eyes. If He takes care of the birds, He will surely take care of you!

# *February 21*

*"Let the children be fed first, for it is not right to take the children's bread and throw it to the dogs."*
**Mark 7:27**

Jesus cares how we treat children. They are to be loved and valued. When a child is mistreated, Jesus is saddened by what He sees. Children need to know that they are loved.

Have you been able to show your love for children? When you love them, Jesus is close. He sees your actions and will reward your obedience. Tell them about Jesus and how much He loves them. Be a doer of the Word by following His command to love.

Jesus has so much love to give. He showers all of us with His love. But the children have a special place in His heart because they are growing and need more love to reach their potential. Who do you know that needs the love of Jesus? Feed them with love and be present in their life today.

# *February 22*

*"I will; be clean."*
*Matthew 8:3*

Jesus will make us clean by His blood. He urges us to come to Him so He can wash us white with grace upon grace. When we draw near to Him, He will draw near to us. He exalts those who humble themselves, and He cleanses those who put their full faith and trust in Him.

Have you put your trust in Jesus? He has been waiting to make you clean. Confess your sins and submit to Him. You are one decision away from healing. Will you take His hand and let Him wash you with the wonder-working power of His blood?

Jesus wants to cover you with His grace. He yearns to see you healed. Why are you still so far away from Him? He is offering you new life when He takes away the stains from sin and puts His seal of redemption upon you. He promises you will be transformed when you take the step toward Him. Come closer, dear one.

# February 23

*"Go home to your friends and tell them how much the Lord has done for you, and how he has had mercy on you."*
**Mark 5:19**

Jesus wants us to tell others that He is full of mercy and grace. He needs us to share our stories so they will know the power of His forgiveness is real. There are people who need to know that they are forgiven. Who can we share our salvation story with today?

Have you written down your testimony so you can remember what the Lord has done for you? Take time and record the ways you have been blessed by His love. Praise Him for the ways He has poured His grace upon you. Be ready, in and out of season, to share what He has done for you.

You are the one He has chosen for such a time as this. He has put His Spirit in you so you can be encouraged by His powerful presence. Go home and tell your friends what a difference He has made in your life. They need to hear your story!

# *February 24*

*"It is written, 'Man shall not live by bread alone.'"*
*Luke 4:4*

We need to pay attention to what God has written down for us in His Word. He gives us instructions so we know how to live according to His will. We cannot live without His loving presence within us. Bread alone will not suffice.

Have you written the words of God on your heart? If you know what is written and do not follow them, you are not living as He commands. If you do not know what is written, it is imperative that you open your Bible and your heart to Him.

Take time and open your Bible. Commit to reading some every day and you will receive His spiritual blessings in abundance. Your food will not be just physical but will be to do the will of God who loves you unconditionally. His spiritual food will satisfy your hunger, and you will be fed by Jesus, the Bread of Life.

# *February 25*

*"Was no one found to return and give praise to God except this foreigner?"*
*Luke 17:18*

God wants us to give Him praise. He asks us to rejoice again and again for who He is and what He is doing in our lives. Remember to rejoice always and give thanks in all circumstances, for this is God's will in Christ Jesus for us.

God is pleased when you speak with positivity and praises. He loves to see you worship even in the hard times. He sees into your soul and loves everything about you, even when you do not love yourself. Let every part of you praise the Lord!

Will you be the one to return and thank God? He is looking far and wide for those who will be thankful and faithful. He knows your thoughts from afar and what is on your mind even before you begin to speak. Shout praises for how awesome God is to you!

# February 26

*"My Father, if this cannot pass unless I drink it, your will be done."*
*Matthew 26:42*

Jesus accepted the Father's will. Even if there was pain and suffering, Jesus was willing to sacrifice all to save us. He wanted a relationship with each of us, so He made the choice to drink the cup that the Father gave to Him. What an amazing Lord we serve!

What cup have you been given? You might be struggling, but God wants you to know that He sees your pain and will take it from you if you release it to Him. He wants to give you peace and yearns for you to find rest for your soul. Take His hand and find refuge in His arms again.

Jesus will get you to the other side. Do you hear Him calling you? Listen to His loving voice trying to get your attention. You have been distracted by so many things. Jesus wants to be the One who leads you home.

# *February 27*

*"But who do you say that I am?"*
*Mark 8:29*

Jesus asks us a very important question when He asks who He is to us. He wants to know if He is our Savior. He wants to be closer to us. He yearns to be our Lord and lives to reach our hearts with His enduring love.

Jesus wants you to love Him and put Him first. He gives you all that you need when you make Him Lord. He showers you with His grace and puts His Spirit in you to empower you. Say yes to Jesus and be blessed, indeed!

Is Jesus still your first love? If so, you will be rewarded with treasures from heaven. If not, He wants you to come back to Him so that He can include you in His kingdom and shower you with the greatest riches you will ever receive. Who do you say Jesus is?

# *February 28*

*"I tell you, in that night there will be two in one bed.
One will be taken and the other left."*
**Luke 17:34**

When Jesus comes back again, those who did not believe will be left behind. They will wonder what happened, when the day comes, and believers are gone. There will be some still here who did not choose to believe but chose their own way. It will be frightening and confusing for those who are left behind.

However, there will be those who go with Jesus when He returns because they did choose to be saved by His grace. He will bring them with Him, and they will go to their heavenly home where they will reside with their Savior, Jesus Christ.

Do you want to be left behind or do you want to be home with Jesus? If you choose to be saved, He will take you with Him when He comes again in glory! All who believe will be raptured with Jesus when He returns and will be with Him forever! It will be a glorious day! Make the choice to believe. You do not want to be left behind!

I HAVE SAID THESE
*things to you,*
THAT IN ME YOU
*may have peace.*
In the world you will
HAVE TRIBULATION.
*But take heart;*
I HAVE OVERCOME
*the world.*
JOHN 16:33

# March 1

*"Surely I am coming soon."*
*Revelation 22:20*

We are promised the good news that Jesus is coming soon. We know this to be true as we wait with anticipation and hope for Him to return. He wants us to keep trusting Him and believe this promise. He yearns to have a close relationship with each of us.

Jesus never stops chasing you. He is with you wherever you go and searches far and wide for hearts who are devoted to Him. Do you have faith even the size of a mustard seed? Have faith, for great is His faithfulness to you.

Keep your eyes open for Jesus. Pray you will keep seeking more of Him until He returns. He is coming soon to bring believers Home with Him. Will you be one of His faithful followers who will go with Him? Be sure you are saved by repenting and inviting Him to live in your heart!

# *March 2*

*"Sanctify them in the truth; your word is truth."*
*John 17:17*

Jesus is praying for us to be set apart in the truth. He wants us to know Him and for His word to be written on our hearts. He prays for His people to be holy and righteous because He loves each of us. He will never stop praying for us!

Do you know that the truth will set you free? Be true to Jesus because He is the truth and the life. He is the only way to the Father. He wants you to be His own, sanctified in the truth, now and forevermore.

Will you trust Jesus without hesitation? Give Him your heart and wait for Him to speak truth to you. He will never let you down. Only Jesus can help you rise, because He reigns above it all. Nothing is too hard for Him!

# *March 3*

*"Ephphatha," that is, "Be opened."*
*Mark 7:34*

Jesus can open hearts. He is the only one who can change us from the inside out. He reaches souls one at a time just in time. He raises dead people back to life with the touch of His healing hand. He positions us where He can restore us with life-giving power.

Do you hear Jesus talking to you? Listen closely with ears to hear Him speaking to you. Place your hand in His and walk with strength where He leads you. He will open up new opportunities for you to serve.

Only Jesus can bring peace where there is hostility and light where there is darkness. Make room for Him in your home by opening the windows to let the light in. You will be able to see all the dust and dirt that needs to be wiped away as you let Him shine on you!

# *March 4*

*"You are the light of the world.*
*A city set on a hill cannot be hidden."*
*Matthew 5:14*

J esus wants us to shine His light for all to see. He does not want us to hide our light but encourages us to stand out like stars in the heavens on a dark night. We can be used for His glory when we lift our praises to the true Light of the world.

Pray about how and where you can you take your candle and light the world so others can see how Jesus has made a difference in your life. Will you share the good news of the gospel with someone today?

Shine, so others can see through the darkness. The brightness in you will illuminate His love. Jesus lives in you, so let the world see how peace is possible through a saving relationship with Jesus Christ.

# *March 5*

*"For to the one who has, more will be given, and from the one who has not, even what he has will be taken away."*
*Mark 4:25*

We receive blessings from above as we give from our heart. God gives bountifully to those who give bountifully. We can be used for His glory as we look to the interests of others.

Jesus sacrificed all so that you could enter into a relationship with Him. He has given you the greatest gift so that you can be free. Do you need to be set free from worry that is weighing on your mind?

Yoke yourself to Jesus and let Him take your burdens. His yoke is easy, and His burden is light. He will give you more rest when you give your worries to Him one at a time. Do not hesitate, but lay it all down at His feet and worship Christ, the true King!

# March 6

*"I tell you, he will give justice to them speedily. Nevertheless, when the Son of Man comes, will he find faith on earth?"*
*Luke 18:8*

Jesus looks far and wide for the faithful. He knows that there is a remnant of people who will remain steadfast until He returns in glory. Everyone who endures to the end will be saved from the wrath to come.

Are you one of His faithful? If so, keep going and do not grow weary in doing good. For at the proper time, you will be exalted and will reap what you sow. He will bring justice speedily to all.

Jesus is looking for the faithful few. Make every effort to be enriched with His love and enlightened with His wisdom by remaining one of the faithful who will be a part of His kingdom of grace. What a glorious day that will be!

# *March 7*

*"Until now you have asked nothing in my name.*
*Ask, and you will receive, that your joy may be full."*
**John 16:24**

We will find joy when we seek more of Jesus. He will give us full joy overlaid with peace when we ask in His name believing that it will be done. As we take our concerns to Him, He not only guides us to all truth, but He brings calm to our souls.

Are you ready to have the joy of Jesus present in you? Ask in the name of Jesus and you will receive the fullness of joy. He is listening and waiting for you to come to Him by faith even when you do not yet see what you hope for.

Open the eyes of your heart. Let the presence of Jesus settle fully in your heart and soul. Give Him all of you so that He can do something new. Only Jesus can turn your weeping into joy! Believe to receive!

# March 8

*"He who has ears to hear, let him hear."*
**Mark 4:9**

Jesus speaks to us when we listen for His voice. His still small voice becomes louder when the other voices in our heads are turned down. The Voice of Truth will triumph over the lies when Jesus is first place in our life.

Whose voice are you listening to? Open your ears so that you may hear. Let the voice of Jesus be the one you follow and obey. He will bring you through it all when you make Him Lord over all.

Close your eyes and open your ears to hear Jesus speaking to you. Pray that His voice will be the one that touches your heart and clears your mind of distractions. You can trust Him to guide you to all truth!

# *March 9*

*"And if anyone forces you to go one mile, go with him two miles."*
**Matthew 5:41**

People might try to force their worldly beliefs on us. At times it will seem as if we are in the minority with our faith. But we are not alone because Jesus is always working in the hearts of His people. Keep planting seeds and stay in the fields for they are ripe for harvest.

Where is Jesus asking you to go that might stretch your faith? He has chosen you to be an ambassador for Him. That conversation He needs you to have will be difficult but remember His faithfulness to you. It is not your job to save people, but to sow seeds of love.

Who has rejected Jesus that you can encourage with love? Love those who persecute you and pray for them. You can keep bringing the light so that someday they will be able to see. It may take time, but when you stay the course, you will be blessed by God's grace.

# March 10

*"Rise, and have no fear."*
*Matthew 17:7*

Fear stops us from doing what we need to do. Fear says no when faith says yes. There are many places in God's Word where He says to have no fear because fear is a liar, and God wants us to live in truth.

Is your faith bigger than your fear? If so, you can rest in His peace. If not, you will fall victim to defeat. Choose faith and rise up with confidence instead of insecurity. The light of the Lord will break forth like the dawn over you for the Lord goes before you.

Honestly ask yourself where you stand now. Does fear or faith rule in you? Then make every effort to trust God at all turns for your faith to rise even more. With faith as your compass, the glory of the Lord will be your rear guard.

# March 11

*"Pay attention to what you hear: with the measure you use, it will be measured to you, and still more will be added to you."*
**Mark 4:24**

Jesus knows our hearts and hears what is on our minds. He also is the first to see how we respond and treat others. Our actions do matter. The way we live does make a difference.

Are you living with Jesus as your firm foundation? Is He the rock on which you stand? When He is, you will love others like He loves you. Only Jesus gives you the power to love because He loved first.

Pray for loving ears to hear what your Savior is telling you. Listen to His love teaching you all things. He is the ultimate judge, not you. He will give and He will take away. Love Him more and you will receive more of His amazing grace that He so freely gives.

# March 12

*"I must preach the good news of the kingdom of God to the other towns as well; for I was sent for this purpose."*
*Luke 4:43*

Jesus preached the good news everywhere He went. He was intentional with His love through His words and His deeds. He calls us to be intentional with our love as well. There are many who need to know how they can be forgiven and free.

Have you considered how Jesus can use you to be a light in His kingdom? He is searching far and wide for those who will be faithful to share the good news of grace through a relationship with Jesus Christ. *He needs you.*

Will you share your story of salvation so that others can know that they, too, can be saved? Jesus loves all and wants all to come to Him. We are all sinners in need of a Savior. You may be that one person who brings someone into the arms of the redeeming grace of Jesus!

# *March 13*

*"Blessed are the merciful,*
*for they shall receive mercy."*
*Matthew 5:7*

We all have sinned and fallen short of the glory of God. We are all sinners in need of forgiveness. Jesus wants to show us how deep and wide His unconditional love is as He gives us grace upon grace.

Will you receive this gift of grace? You do not deserve it, but it is yours because the Father gave you His Son so that you can have a saving relationship with Him through Jesus. He died and rose again so that you can live in freedom!

Pray that you will choose to give mercy even when it is not deserved. Think of how much mercy you have been given. He blesses the merciful with even more mercy. Will you choose mercy? It is your choice to give and receive, so make the decision today to shine for God's glory!

# March 14

*"To you has been given the secret of the kingdom of God, but for those outside everything is in parables."*
**Mark 4:11**

The secret of the kingdom of God is for all who believe. It is for us to share. We will know when we believe. When we are close to God, He reveals the secret. When we are on the outside, we will not fully understand.

Where are you? Do you believe or are you chasing myths? Jesus is the only way. He is the way, the truth, and the life. He is calling you into relationship with Him. Only Jesus can take you to the Father.

What is keeping you from fully surrendering? Jesus Christ has come so that all who believe will be saved. He is just a prayer away from your reach. Pray that you will take His hand and let Him save you by your surrender of your will to His. He loves you so much!

# March 15

*"Truly, I say to you, there are some standing here who will not taste death until they see the kingdom of God after it has come with power."*
**Mark 9:1**

Jesus promises that some will see the kingdom of God without tasting death. This is difficult to wrap our heads around, but knowing it is true makes us love our Lord even more. He wants all to be saved. He will come in all power and glory, and we will see what has been promised to us!

Do you believe? Make the choice to believe without seeing. Let your faith rise to new heights with the Father who loves you so much that He gave His Son so that all who believe will not perish but have everlasting life.

Now that you believe, come to His throne of grace and sit at the feet of Jesus. He wants you to stop being so busy that you cannot hear what He is telling you. Jesus loves to teach you and is waiting for you to activate the Holy Spirit living in you so that you can know the power of His love.

# March 16

*"This is he of whom it is written, 'Behold, I send my messenger before your face, who will prepare your way before you."*
**Luke 7:27**

Jesus wants to get our attention. He seeks to share truth with us. He has prepared the way for us by sending His messenger to go before Him who will share the hope that exists with Jesus. When we listen, trust, and obey, we will be blessed, indeed.

Our sweet Savior brings His sacrificial love to you. There is no greater love that can be given than by one who lays down His life for His friends. Jesus values you and has laid down His life for *you*.

How will you respond to His love? Jesus wants to reach you with the good news that he has overcome the world. He who is greater in you has conquered death so that you will live. This is the greatest news ever!

# March 17

*"The time is fulfilled, and the kingdom of God is at hand; repent and believe in the gospel."*
*Mark 1:15*

It is time to truly believe. It is beyond time for us to see that God is at hand in our lives. He has been with us, and we have not recognized Him actively living in us because we are bombarded by our own voices in our minds.

His will is for you to repent and believe. He wants you to turn away from the lies you believe in and turn to Him, the Voice of Truth. When you do, you will know the truth and He will set you free!

Do you want to be free from the guilt you are carrying around? Let go and ask for Jesus to forgive you. Then come to the fountain of life and drink the water from Jesus so you will not be thirsty again. His living water will refresh and revive you!

# March 18

*"Can the wedding guests mourn as long as the
bridegroom is with them? The days will come when
the bridegroom is taken away from them, and then
they will fast."*
*Matthew 9:15*

Jesus was telling His friends to be present with
Him. He wanted them to have joy because He
was with them. When we keep our eyes fixed on
Jesus and our hearts close to His, He will infuse us
with greater joy! He lives in us!

Do not let your hearts be troubled by earthly
problems. These things meant to harm you can be the
fertile soil to grow your faith. Jesus is still with you
wherever you go. He sees what you are going through
and will attend to the voice of your prayers. Call upon
Him in faith, believing that He does care about you
and will help you.

Have you given your burdens to Jesus? Close your
eyes and breathe in His grace and love and He will
strengthen you for what you are going through. Only
Jesus can take away the pain and replace it with joy.
There is joy in the journey when you journey with
Jesus!

# March 19

*"Talitha cumi," which means,*
*"Little girl, I say to you, arise."*
**Mark 5:41**

We will be healed when we trust Jesus. He will wake us up and lift us up because only He knows the things that keep pressing us down. He needs us to keep praying, knowing that there is still hope for us. We do not have to be afraid when Jesus is on our side.

He will be your refuge and strength and a very present help in trouble. He will attend to the voice of your prayers. Listen to Him calling you into relationship with Him. Rise up and come to Jesus.

Will you rise when Jesus calls your name? He needs you to get up and grow your faith so you can bloom where He has planted you. He will bless you as you trust Him more. Take heart, for Jesus sees your faith and will heal you from head to toe.

# *March 20*

*"Will you lay down your life for me? Truly, truly, I say to you, the rooster will not crow till you have denied me three times."*
**John 13:38**

Jesus is our life and is right by our side. He wants us to lay down our life for Him by continuing to trust Him knowing that He makes all things new. When life seems to be pulling us away from Jesus, He wants us to come closer to Him so He can restore us again.

Have you recognized Jesus working in you? He wants to be active in you so that you can live with the power of the Holy Spirit. Only Jesus can make all things new when you trust Him and let Him have His way in you.

Come to the fountain of life where you will be refreshed again. Give Jesus your hand so you can grow spiritually with Him. He will place new opportunities in your life so that His light will illuminate your way and His living water will revive your soul.

# March 21

*"What man of you, having a hundred sheep, if he has lost one of them, does not leave the ninety-nine in the open country, and go after the one that is lost, until he finds it?"*
*Luke 15:4*

Jesus will run after us until He finds us. He knows how we need Him. Only Jesus can give us all that we need because He loves us. He will never forsake us but will renew our hearts and minds in Him.

Do you feel lost? Take heart, because Jesus loves you and sees you. He will give you all that you need as you trust Him, again and again. Jesus is the answer to your questions and the way to the Father. Give Him your whole heart and you will see the way out of your mess.

Do you hear Him whispering your name? He will call you until He finds you. Only Jesus sees what you are really going through and will comfort you in all times. The problems you are facing are difficult, but with Jesus as your compass and guide, you will never be lost again!

# *March 22*

*"Beware of the scribes, who like to walk around in long robes and like greetings in the marketplaces."*
*Mark 12:38*

Jesus does not like the proud and haughty. He will humble those who exalt themselves. He will bring the proud to their knees. He wants us to be humble and kind and beware of those who condemn and judge others.

Jesus will protect you from people who try to hurt you by their idle gossip and lies. They will never touch you when Jesus is Lord of your life. They will try to bring you down but will never succeed, because the Lord will fight for you. You only have to be silent.

Stay humble and walk righteously before your Lord so that at the proper time He may exalt you. He sees what is happening and knows the truth. Jesus always prevails. Rely on Him and you will soar with wings like eagles!

# March 23

*"His master said to him, 'Well done, good and faithful servant. You have been faithful over a little; I will set you over much. Enter into the joy of your master.'"*
*Matthew 25:21*

Jesus rewards those who stay faithful. In fact, He will give more to those who stay faithful. When we are faithful in just a little, He will set us over much more. Enter into the joy of the master by staying the course and remaining one of His faithful few.

Where is Jesus calling you to be faithful? Maybe you have heard His voice but are letting fear stop you. He wants to bless your life with joy, so listen and do what He is calling you to do. He will set you over much when you stay faithful over a little.

Joy exists with Jesus. Peace is found in His presence. Put Him first in your life and do what He calls you to do, and He will bless your heart with these beautiful words, "Well done, good and faithful servant."

# *March 24*

*"Ask, and it will be given to you; seek, and you will find; knock, and it will be opened to you."*
*Matthew 7:7*

When we ask, Jesus answers. When we seek, we will find. When we knock, it will be opened to us. Only Jesus can give us all that we need. Ask, seek, and knock to find His blessings.

Have you asked for what is on your heart? Do not stop seeking Jesus and praying for what you need. He is listening and watching you. He is reaching down to open the door so you can find Him on the other side.

That issue you are facing is real, but Jesus is the way to overcome it. He loves you so much and needs you to remain close to Him so that He can shine the light over the situation and give you much needed peace. Seek more of Him so that He can give you the desires of your heart.

# March 25

*"For nothing is hidden except to be made manifest;*
*nor is anything secret except to come to light."*
**Mark 4:22**

Secrets are not secret to Jesus. He sees, He knows, He loves. He wants us to confess and repent so that we can come closer to His love. He forgives and sets us free when we come out of the dark and into His glorious light!

Examine yourself and see where you need to ask forgiveness. Jesus will show you the things that you are trying to hide. He will forgive you when you ask. Remember that Jesus has sacrificed all so that you can be forgiven and free.

Pray that you will stop hiding and come out of the dark. If you stay close to Him, Jesus will remove you from the sin that keeps you pressed down and stressed. He will wipe away every tear and take away every fear. Trust Him and ask for Him to rescue you because He will surely do it!

# March 26

*"Sit here while I pray."*
**Mark 14:32**

Why are we always too busy running around that we cannot sit with Jesus? Life gets in the way when we stay away from Savior. But Jesus has saving grace for us even when we are too distracted. He is there for us even when we are too busy for Him. Stay close to Jesus and pray.

Jesus shows you how important it is to pray. He spoke to the Father all the time by taking time to pray. He knew that His prayers would bring Him close to the Father. He wants you to pray. Have you prayed today?

Be still and talk to Jesus. Let Him in your heart and listen to what He speaks to you. He will attend to the voice of your prayers and answer in His will and timing. Take heart and make time for Jesus to speak to you. It is time to pray!

# March 27

*My Father is working until now,*
*and I am working."*
*John 5:17*

We cannot always see our Father working, but know that He is doing more around us than we can dream or imagine. He will show us great wonders as we look for Him with eyes wide open.

Are you living with eyes to see? Look around you and notice the beautiful colors that Jesus brings when you live with the Spirit in you. He enhances your ordinary life with extraordinary power.

Think about how dull your life would be without Jesus. Thank Him for all He has done for you and is doing now in your life. He will work all things out in His timing and in His special way to brighten your days.

# March 28

*"I have said these things to you, that in me you may*
*have peace. In the world you will have tribulation.*
*But take heart; I have overcome the world."*
*John 16:33*

Jesus knows that we will face things that may
bring us down, but He wants us to take heart and
not be troubled because He has overcome the
world. Jesus is the Prince of Peace and through Him
we will have peace if we remain in Him.

Are you searching for peace? Look to Jesus, and He
will give you the peace you need. Take a moment
today and let His peace wash over you. He will calm
your heart with His gentle Spirit.

Forget the worries that are holding you captive. He
will remove the hardships and strongholds if you let
Him carry your burdens. There is nothing that is too
hard for Him. Hear the chains falling to the ground?

# March 29

*"You have heard that it was said, 'You shall love your neighbor and hate your enemy."*
*Matthew 5:43*

The world tells us to hate our enemies, but what does Jesus say? He says to love our neighbors and pray for our enemies so as to show honor to Him. He loves all of us and wants us to live in love with all people. It might seem hard to do, but with Jesus as our pilot, we can love with certainty.

Do you have a hard time loving those who come against you? Jesus knows how you are feeling. He was persecuted and pushed aside but sacrificed His life so that we may have life and have it abundantly.

Will you forgive those who persecute you and try to steal your joy? There will be some who try to make you feel unwanted and unworthy, but they will not prevail when Jesus is on your side. Seek Him while He is near to you.

# March 30

*"A prophet is not without honor, except in his hometown and among his relatives and in his own household."*
*Mark 6:4*

We might not know how much Jesus loves us until we think about how much He went through for us. He was bruised, crushed, condemned, and cursed by many. Even those closest to Him did not believe Him. It is hard to fathom that our Savior could not even convince those in His own household that He was the Son of God.

Do you have a hard time talking to your family about Jesus? If so, keep showing them Jesus by your actions of love and grace. Keep praying for them to know the truth and never give up on them. There will be a day when your efforts will be rewarded by the great I AM.

Is it a struggle to tell those in your circle how Jesus has changed your life? Do not let your fear of what they might think stop you from sharing. The more you speak about Jesus, the deeper your faith will grow. Eventually you will see what you hoped for if you just believe!

# March 31

*"I am the Alpha and the Omega, the first and the last, the beginning and the end."*
*Revelation 22:13*

Jesus is the beginning of all things and the end of all things. He will be the one who has the final word. He speaks truth into being and life unto death. When we put our full faith and trust in Him, He will be our all in all, once and for all.

Do you know Jesus is for you and not against you? Others may come against you, but not Jesus. He is the same yesterday, today, and always. He will not give up on you, so never give up on Him.

What are you facing that seems too difficult to handle? Give Jesus the wheel and let Him drive you to the place where there is no more fear. With Jesus, there is true victory over anything or anyone. He reigns, forever and ever!

AND YOU WILL
KNOW THE TRUTH,
*and the truth*
will set you free.
JOHN 8:32

# April 1

*"For John baptized with water, but you will be
baptized with the Holy Spirit not many days from
now."*
*Acts 1:5*

Jesus wants to fill us with His Spirit and will do so
when we come to Jesus with a repentant heart
ready to receive His spiritual power. We will be
born again with Jesus and raised from death to life as
we commit ourselves to Jesus. Our baptism is an
outward sign of how much we love Jesus and how we
want to follow Him and dedicate our lives to Him.

Are you ready to let go of the old and put on the new?
He wants to meet you where you are and greet you
with His grace. He knows the weight you are carrying
is heavy and burdensome. He will lift it from you
with one simple touch of His Spirit.

Will you make the choice to live with His spiritual
power? It is impossible to experience joy and peace
without Jesus centermost in your life. If you are
ready, He is waiting. He would love to make you His.
Take off your old self and put on your new self,
created in perfection by the Father through faith in
Jesus Christ. Then you will be ready to be baptized
with the Holy Spirit.

# April 2

*"Stretch out your hand."*
**Mark 3:5**

The world needs love. People are hurting and cannot find peace because of all the hate that exists. But Jesus, full of mercy and grace, will heal all who come to Him. He wants us to come to the foot of the cross and to lay it all down. When we do, we will find healing and peace.

Are you ready to be healed? Stretch out your hand to reach Jesus who commands healing in His name. He brings life to death and light to darkness. The light of the world will illuminate your life when you let Him in. He fills the empty places of your soul and brings healing to your heart.

Come seek Jesus for what you need. Give Him your heart so He can revive you with His healing peace. Talk to Him and tell Him what you need. He is listening and will attend to the voice of your prayers anytime you call upon Him.

# April 3

*"Repent, for the kingdom of heaven is at hand."*
*Matthew 4:17*

Jesus calls us to repent and believe because the kingdom of heaven is at hand. He wants all to come to Him so that we can be saved. It is clear that He is near to all who call upon Him in truth. He takes our sorrows and turns them to joy the day we turn away from sin and turn toward His beautiful face.

Are you letting His face shine down on you and give you peace? See Him smiling at you, dear one. He knows how much you need Him right now and will comfort you after your loss. He does not want you to dwell in sadness but wants you to walk in sunshine.

Will you turn toward His face? He sees you and loves you. Lean on His true forgiveness and not your regret. It is time to turn towards Jesus and walk away from those things that are making you feel guilty. Come closer and be set free, once and for all!

# *April 4*

*"And whenever you stand praying, forgive, if you
have anything against anyone, so that your Father
also who is in heaven may forgive you your
trespasses."*
*Mark 11:25*

Jesus wants us to forgive others. He promises to
forgive us when we forgive others their
trespasses. He knows it is hard to forgive but
needs us to pray and then choose forgiveness and not
bitterness. Our Father in heaven will forgive us when
we forgive.

Who do you need to forgive? Say their names and tell
God you forgive them. When you do, the peace of
forgiveness will pass over you. It depends on you. Be
a peacemaker and you will experience the peace that
passes all understanding.

Tell Jesus how special He is to you. Spend time
worshipping Him with gratitude for your forgiveness.
Talk to the One who truly forgives without strings
attached. He is the Prince of Peace and the way to
freedom because He rushes in with saving grace to
love all sinners.

# *April 5*

*"I tell you, this man went down to his house justified, rather than the other. For everyone who exalts himself will be humbled, but the one who humbles himself will be exalted."*
*Luke 18:14*

Will we choose to humble ourselves before Jesus so that He can do His work in us? The proud will not see all that Jesus can do in them because they will be looking only at themselves. But the humble will be exalted and be able to work for His glory. Jesus is looking for the humble so that He can work mightily in them.

Will you be one of the humble ones? He is looking far and wide for those who can be lifted up. There is much work left to be done. He wants to begin a new thing in you. Do you understand what He is speaking to you?

Finish the work He has begun in you with your eyes fixed on Jesus Christ. He is the prize you have been seeking and the joy set before you. His death on the cross is proof of His love for you. Love His mercy and walk humbly before your God!

# April 6

*"As you sent me into this world, so I have sent them into the world."*
**John 17:18**

Jesus prays for His children. He loves to set them apart by sending them into the world to shine as lights in the world. As we are sent, we go with courage and blessing from Him. He will never leave us alone but will encourage us with His prayers and promises.

Jesus was sent to save the lost. He ransomed His life so that you would have life and have it in abundance. He was born so that you could be born again. Tell Jesus how much you love Him and then show Him by setting an example of how to love as He has loved you.

Who can you love right now that needs a little encouragement and building up? Think of someone who the Lord puts on your heart and pray for them. There are so many who just need a little more love, and Jesus has sent you to share His love. He is cheering you on!

# April 7

*"And behold, I am coming soon. Blessed is the one who keeps the words of the prophecy of this book."*
*Revelation 22:7*

Jesus is coming soon! Take heart, do not be afraid. Watch for the signs of His return with eagerness and hope. He will come in glory and bring Home those who believe in Him. Read the Bible and realize that the prophecy is clearer and nearer than when we first believed.

Are you keeping the words of the prophecy of the Bible? He is calling you to wait upon Him with eyes to see and ears to hear. Jesus is coming soon! Make sure you are one of His faithful followers so that you will be with Him in paradise. He will take those who follow Him to be with Him forever!

The thief on the cross asked Jesus to remember Him after he died. Jesus told him that he would be with Him because He wanted to be saved. He believed Jesus was the Son of God. Jesus is coming soon! Do you believe? Make sure that you do, so you can experience all that Jesus promises to those who believe.

# *April 8*

*"The kingdom of God is as if a man should scatter
seed on the ground."*
*Mark 4:26*

We are called to plant seeds for Jesus. He needs us to step out and sow seeds of hope into hearts so that people may know His love. The fields are ready for seed sowing so they may be harvested. People will know more about Jesus by our love. Keep planting, so the seeds will keep growing.

People will begin to open their hearts more when the seeds you plant start sprouting. You can watch the love you plant bloom beautifully and magically. Just keep planting, and God will water for the growth to happen.

Will you be a farmer for Jesus by having Jesus conversations with people? Just a simple act of kindness will plant life into them, and they will smell the sweet aroma of Jesus. Make every moment count and every conversation matter for His glory. Scatter seed wherever you go.

# April 9

*"Our friend Lazarus has fallen asleep,
but I go to awaken him."*
*John 11:11*

Jesus gives us new life when we awaken to His truth. We wake up when we obey Him and trust His hand to lead us wherever we go. His peace is simply perfect because He will never leave or forsake us even when we take our eyes off of Him. He is always with us.

Where are your eyes? Are you looking for Jesus knowing that He is seeking after you? Give Him another chance to restore you. Let Him bring life back into the parts of you that need revived. Look up, dear one, because Jesus is reaching for you.

Jesus can raise the dead and bring them life. Trust Jesus to give *you* life once again. Do not be afraid to give Him your hand so He can raise you up. Repent, rise up, and be made alive with Christ in you!

# April 10

***"And you will know the truth,
and the truth will set you free."***
***John 8:32***

J esus is the way, the truth, and the life. When we know the truth, He will set us free. No one comes to the Father except through Him. When we come to Jesus, He will make a way for us to know the Father and the Holy Spirit will dwell in us.

Are you still seeking truth other places rather than with Jesus? If so, you will not find the truth. He promises truth to those who call upon Him. He gives life to those who call Him friend and Savior.

Have you looked to the Lord who is faithful to you? Listen to Him so that He can share truth with you. He has been trying to share with you, but you have been ignoring Him. Only Jesus can bring truth to your life, so always trust Him.

# April 11

*"I am no longer worthy to be called your son
Treat me as one of your hired servants."*
**Luke 15:19**

There are times where we do not feel worthy. We feel the weight of our sins and do not know where to turn. Jesus knows how we feel and wants us to listen to His comforting voice calling us closer to Him.

When you feel unsure and insecure, where do you turn? Jesus wants you to turn to Him and seek Him for all you need. He brightens your path and blesses your steps when you stay in line with Him and do not let others bring you down.

Jesus wants you to be His, so let your guard down and give Him all your worries and fears. He will give you all you need. Trust His plan and open your hands. He will lift you up and bring you through it.

# April 12

*"If you then, who are evil, know how to give good gifts to your children, how much more will your Father who is in heaven give good things to those who ask him!"*
*Matthew 7:11*

Jesus wants to give good gifts to us. He yearns for us to call upon Him so He can give us what we need. But why are we too afraid to ask Him for what we need? He will bless us because He loves to give good gifts to His children.

What do you need? Have you asked the Father who is in heaven? He delights to give you all that you need and enjoys seeing you basking in His goodness and glory. He will not lead you astray but will encourage your heart with His tokens of love.

Seek the Lord for His blessings. He will listen to your heart because He knows what you really need. Only Jesus can bless you richly with His gifts that He gives generously. The gifts of the world are temporary and will not last like the gifts from the Father. Ask, and you shall receive, indeed!

# *April 13*

*"From the fig tree learns its lesson: as soon as its branch becomes tender and puts out its leaves, you know that summer is near."*
*Mark 13:28*

Tender mercies are all around us. We might not notice what Jesus is doing because we are simply too busy. The trees are growing right before our very eyes, and we do not even see them changing. The flowers are blooming beautifully, and we are too distracted to smell their aroma or see the newest blossoms.

But, when you look around you with eyes to see, there will be things that appear out of nowhere to brighten your world and change your perspective. These things are from Jesus who makes everything beautiful in its time. He will show you great and mighty things that make your day brighter.

Are you looking around you so that you can see? Discover that His mercies are new every morning and His promises are true all the time. There is no place you can escape His love and tenderness. When Jesus is your Savior, His goodness reigns in you and you will see!

# *April 14*

"*It is written, 'My house shall be a house of prayer,
but you have made it a den of robbers.'*"
*Luke 19:46*

P rayer is so special to the Lord. He wants us to take time to pray to Him. Do we make time to go to His house to worship and pray? He needs us to make time to pray every day so He can speak to us. We will hear Him when we decide to open our hearts and pray.

Have you noticed the people who stop and pray no matter what comes their way? If you do not neglect to pray, but make it an important part of your day, you will see more of what God can do in your life. He loves it when His people choose to pray.

Prayer is the path to communication with Jesus. He hears you as you let your requests be made known to Him. He will respond to you with joy as you pray. Do you want your prayers answered? If so, then pray and be filled with utmost joy from knowing that your Lord hears you and will answer no matter where or when you pray!

# April 15

*"I can do nothing on my own. As I hear, I judge,
and my judgment is just, because I seek not my own
will but the will of him who sent me."*
***John 5:30***

Jesus seeks to please the Father and to do His will
and not His own. He wants His Father to know
how much He loves Him so He obeys His
commands and follows His will. He can do nothing
on His own without the Father.

Do you realize that you can do nothing without the
Father? He needs you to listen so He can show you
what He desires and what His will is for you. Jesus
wants you to see Him lovingly following the will of
the Father so that you will make the choice to do His
will as well.

Take heart and know that the will of the Father is so
good. Only the Father knows what is best and when
you do His will, His judgment will be just for you.
Seek the things that are above where Jesus is seated at
the right hand of the Father, and you, too, will be
doing the will of the Father who is so good to you all
the time.

# *April 16*

*"If you abide in me, and my words abide in you, ask whatever you wish, and it will be done for you."*
*John 15:7*

Jesus wants us to abide in Him so He can tell us what He needs for us to do. His will for us is to abide in Him. Abiding is the way we can know what He wants for us. Abide in Him so that His will can be done.

Are you still trying to figure out what Jesus' will is for you? Try abiding in Him so that He can show you. There are many opportunities for you to see Him, but only when He is first in your life. Seek Him and live in love.

Jesus speaks to you when you open the door to your heart and let His love flow in and through you. Abiding in Jesus is loving Him completely as you seek Him with all your heart. You will find Jesus as you seek Him and listen for His declarations of love.

# April 17

*"But when you pray, go into your room and shut the*
*door and pray to your Father who is in secret. And*
*your Father who sees in secret will reward you."*
**Matthew 6:6**

The times we meet the Father in prayer are very sacred to Him. He sees us praying in our secret place where our prayers reach Him. Time after time He meets us where we pray. He listens for our voice and answers with His.

Go and shut the door and pray so that the Father can reward you. He has been waiting to hear your prayers in your secret place of prayer. It is always so good to hear Him. Go and pray so that you can know what He desires for you.

As you pray, listen so you know how to respond to Him. He reaches those who touch Him with their prayers. The power of prayer is real and will be the perfect way you can hear and respond to the powerful presence of your Father. Pray, because your Defender is waiting to hold you in His strong arms.

# April 18

*"It is like a grain of mustard seed, which, when sown on the ground, is the smallest of all the seeds on earth."*
**Mark 4:31**

Jesus compared faith to a grain of mustard seed. It is the smallest of seeds on the earth, but can grow into one of the biggest trees to provide needed shelter to many birds. Similarly, the smallest amount of faith can produce in us the greatest faith when we cling to Jesus the perfecter of our faith.

Where do you need to grow your faith? Even the smallest faith can produce great rewards for you. Without faith, it is impossible to please God. He wants you to keep growing so that He can use you in His kingdom to help others know Him. He is the vine, and you are the branches to spread His love.

Abide in Jesus and you can see your faith sprout new growth and give hope to you and those around you. Everyone needs to know Jesus and He can use you to reach the dying world with the sweet aroma of His grace. Will you bloom new faith where Jesus has planted you?

# *April 19*

*"And blessed is the one who is not offended by me."*
*Luke 7:23*

We are blessed when we share and do not shy away from spreading the good news of Jesus Christ with others. Jesus needs us to show the world how His love saves and that His way is the only way to true freedom and peace. What the world needs is more love.

Do you feel offended because someone hurt your feelings? Jesus knows what it is like to be persecuted and shamed. He wants you to let it go and know that with Jesus in the driver's seat, He will fight your battles. Only Jesus can take the pain and put His seal of joy on you.

Take the offense and throw it off you. Jesus will take it from you when you are ready. Give Jesus your heart and let Him show you how His love can change hearts and minds and give you the courage to let go. He is waiting and ready to bless your troubled heart.

# *April 20*

*Why are you troubled,*
*and why do doubts arise in your hearts?"*
*Luke 24:38*

We have the power of the Holy Spirit available to us when we become a follower of Jesus. Only Jesus can give us the hope we need when we turn to Him and let Him seal us with the power of His Spirit. He knows that doubts will arise in our hearts but promises to calm us and show us the way.

The storm you are facing has put doubts in your heart. You are torn about what to do in these uncertain times and Jesus sees how you are responding. Rest assured that He can provide a better way for you. Take time to make Him your first priority.

When you look to Jesus and keep basking in the light of His love, He will give you the clarity you are seeking. He will take away the trial and light a fire for Him in your heart once again. Will you trust the Light of the World to fan a flame in you?

# April 21

"God is spirit, and those who worship him must
worship in spirit and truth."
John 4:24

Those who worship God know Him well. True worshippers will worship Him in spirit and truth. God looks for those who will worship Him this way. We have opportunities to spend time with God as we praise Him for who He is and what He has done for us.

Praising God is part of the way you express your gratitude to Him. Are you thanking God instead of complaining about what you do not have? He wants your praise and blesses those who keep Him close. Lift up your praise and let go of your worries and you will see what a difference He makes in your life.

Do you worship the Father in spirit and truth? Try praising Him for all the things He has done for you. Take a moment and thank Him for all His blessings. Count these many blessings and name them one by one and you will see all that God has done.

# *April 22*

*"Neither will I tell you by what authority I do these things."*
*Mark 11:33*

All authority has been given to Jesus from God. He knows what He is doing and how things will be done. It is not for us to know the details, but it is time for us to say yes and give up the fight for control. It is in the surrender that our Savior stands with us.

When you stand firm, Jesus conquers your fears and takes away your insecurities. With Jesus, you only need to be silent. He saves those who draw close to Him and brings peace to any situation. Jesus is there for you and promises to give you all that you need.

Do you need strength for the battle you are facing? Ask Jesus who will hear your battle cry and fight for you. Lean on Him and He will rescue you, again and again. There is victory in Jesus, your Savior, forever!

# *April 23*

*"If the world hates you, know that it has hated me before it hated you."*
**John 15:18**

Jesus knows that unfortunately we will experience hatred just like those who hated Him. But Jesus tells us that we will be blessed when others revile us because He promises to lift us up especially in those times. Look for the rainbows He brings after the storms.

Do not give the haters any attention, but turn your eyes to the love of Jesus. He will bring silver linings in the midst of your problems. Reach for Jesus and He will bring you out of the storm.

Are you more focused on the storms around you or on the Savior guiding you? When you stay close to Jesus, peace will permeate every part of your life including the times you face trials and tribulations. Turn your eyes upon Jesus and look at His beautiful face.

# April 24

*"The Spirit of the Lord is upon me, because he has anointed me to proclaim good news to the poor. He has sent me to proclaim liberty to the captives and recovering of sight to the blind, to set at liberty those who are oppressed, to proclaim the year of the Lord's favor."*
*Luke 4:18*

Jesus proclaims the Lord's favor for us all. He proclaims good news to the poor, brings liberty to the captives and the oppressed, and gives sight to the blind. He grants peace to all who seek Him and He lives inside those who love Him.

The Spirit of the Lord is upon Jesus Christ. His power dwells in those who choose to follow Him. Will you make the choice to invite Jesus into your heart? When you do, He will surround you with shouts of joy and pearls of wisdom from heaven above.

Are you seeking the peace of Jesus? Trust Him so that He can place peace that passes all understanding inside of you. He will never let you down or leave you because He loves you with an everlasting love. Believe that He loves you and shout His praises with joy!

# April 25

*"Do not think that I have come to bring peace to the earth. I have not come to bring peace, but a sword."*
*Matthew 10:34*

The cares of the world can overwhelm us. People can betray us. Situations can steal our joy. But Jesus came to conquer all. He will fight for us all the time. We only need to be still so He can work miracles for us.

Do you need to step out of the way so Jesus can step in? He will bring His sword to the battlefront so that our enemies will be defeated. Stand tall with Jesus so those who come against you will fall flat on their face. He will bring justice where He finds injustice.

Count on Jesus to rescue you. Know that He can make your enemies His footstool and stomp out the negativity. Rely on His Spirit to give you power to get you out of the situation that has brought you down. The way up and out is through Jesus Christ!

# *April 26*

*"Truly, I say to you, one of you will betray me, one who is eating with me."*
**Mark 14:18**

Jesus knew who would betray Him. He saw the one who would take from Him and He knew how it would happen. His thoughts are higher than ours and His ways are greater. Jesus knows all of us and what we are thinking.

Are you praising Jesus for your blessings or complaining about what you do not have? He hears you and knows what you are thinking. He wants to see you praising Him even in the challenges you are facing. He yearns to talk to you when you are ready to listen.

Spend some time in prayer and hear His voice. Jesus is ready to tell you some great and mighty things that you have not known. He is anxious to spend some time with you today. Have you made time for Jesus?

# April 27

*"Rise and go your way;*
*your faith has made you well."*
*Luke 17:19*

Healing comes in God's perfect timing and His will. We will find healing for our hearts when we enter into thanksgiving for all He is doing in our lives. All His blessings will fall upon us as we keep seeking Him faithfully and fervently knowing that He is there for us all the time.

Have you asked for God's healing believing that He is able to heal you? God wants to see your faith. He yearns to know you better. He watches and waits for you to ask Him for what is on your heart. He hears you praising Him even before the healing takes place.

Remember that God is faithful all the time. He never fails you. Reach out and ask Him for the healing you are seeking. Give Him your heart so that He can infuse you with courage and strength to get through your challenges. He knows exactly what you need even before you ask Him. He is listening, so ask, and you shall receive so that your joy may be full!

# *April 28*

*"As you enter the house, greet it."*
*Matthew 10:12*

What if we all chose greetings instead of grumblings? The world would be a better place if people shared love and not hate and were united and not divided. Jesus tells us to love and build others up. He wants us to encourage those He puts in our lives.

Ponder the ways Jesus can use you to love others. Where is He calling you? If you are not sure, ask Him to show you. He will bring you to those who He needs you to touch with His love. There are hearts waiting to be transformed by the perfect love of the Savior.

Only Jesus can save and heal. He is the one who will never leave or forsake you. He has given you indications about where you can be used for His glory, so go and greet where He places you. Be a light who will direct others to find salvation and freedom in Jesus Christ. He is counting on you!

# *April 29*

*"Truly, truly, I say to you,
I am the door of the sheep."*
**John 10:7**

Jesus is the door of the sheep ready to let us in His sheepfold. He wants to guard us and help us. He will watch over us and protect us from those who try to come against us. Come to the One who always keeps us safe.

Do you want to be protected? Turn to Jesus so that He can open the door for you. He sees you and wants to keep His eyes on you. Hear His voice calling you to that safe haven where He is. Jesus will protect you always. He is the same today, yesterday, and forever.

Only Jesus can bring you out of the difficult situation that is before you. He needs you to trust Him to get you out of that bind. He can rescue you from whatever you are going through. Nothing is too hard for Him. Will you let Him put you where He can encircle you with His love?

# April 30

*"Whoever seeks to preserve his life will lose it,*
*but whoever loses his life will keep it."*
**Luke 17:33**

When we let it all go and give it all to Jesus, we will have abundant life. He wants to give us a life of joy and freedom. He yearns for us to let go of what the world wants us to keep holding onto so we can find what really matters. We will find Jesus when we lose our life.

Lose your life and you will find Him. When you decrease, He will increase in you. Jesus loves to give life to those who will take up their cross and follow Him. Will you be one of the followers of Jesus?

Jesus promises to lead you in the mountains and in the valleys. He will never turn away from you but will bring you through it if He takes you to it. What are you facing that seems too daunting? Lose your life for the sake of Jesus and He will give you more than you could ever dream or imagine.

TAKE HEART
*daughter*
YOUR FAITH
*has made you*
well.
MATTHEW 9:22

# May 1

*"Take heart, daughter;*
*your faith has made you well."*
**Matthew 9:22**

We all need the healing touch of Jesus. When we believe, He tenderly heals our hearts. He knows our hearts and knows them very well. Our strength increases as He increases in us. When we are in need of His peace, He places it right in the center of our heart and soul where we find restoration.

Are you looking for healing? Take heart and open your heart to Jesus. He has much to show you, for He knows what is on your heart. He is close to you, so draw near to Him and He will draw near to you. Only Jesus can take you through the storm you are facing. Only Jesus can bring healing to the deep places where pain resides.

Do you see what He is trying to show you? This situation you are facing is the perfect opportunity to grow your faith and dive deeper into a relationship with Jesus. He is ready to help you navigate this as you take hold of His hand and open your heart to His love. Jesus is the way, the truth, and the life. Come to Him and you will be healed in His presence!

# May 2

*"You lack one thing: go, sell all that you have and give to the poor, and you will have treasure in heaven; and come, follow me."*
*Mark 10:21*

Treasures in heaven are found when we look to Jesus. He gives us opportunities to find those things when He is our first love. Only Jesus knows what we should give to the poor and He hopes that we will follow Him and follow through. As we obey Him, he opens the heavens for us to see what really matters.

What do you need to relinquish so that Jesus can work in you? Ask Him to show you what He needs you to do and be determined to give with a generous spirit. He wants you to believe He can work miracles through you. He yearns for you to be ready in and out of season to share what He has put on your heart.

Where can you bless Jesus by using your gifts? Take time and ask Him, knowing He will show you how you can be a blessing. Follow Him where He leads you and be careful how you spend your days. Every day is a gift for you to come closer to the One who created you. He is shining in and through you for His glory!

# May 3

*"Now is my soul troubled. And what shall I say? 'Father, save me from this hour'? But for this purpose I have come to this hour."*
**John 12:27**

We all will face troubles. We know our Father knows what is before us. But He will give us courage to keep going when we keep Him close and ask for His direction and power. Do not fear when these troubles intersect your path because Jesus will take what is meant for harm and use it for good.

Remember the promises and receive each one with gladness and joy. Jesus has wonderful things to show you as you wait. He cannot take his eye off you so keep your eye on Him. He has crafted plans for you that will take you to your purpose.

Jesus took your pain and suffered for you. He gave His life so you could have freedom from sin and comfort in the hard times. He knows you and loves every part of you, dear one. There is nothing that you have done that will make Him love you less. Reach out and touch Him and let Him cover you with His gentle wings.

# *May 4*

"*But you will receive power when the Holy Spirit has come upon you, and you will be my witnesses in Jerusalem and in all Judea and Samaria, and to the end of the earth.*"
*Acts 1:8*

As we surrender all to Jesus, the Spirit manifests Himself to us and dwells in us. We will receive this power when the Holy Spirit comes upon us. We will receive all when we believe because He is alive in our hearts. Be a witness by living in the working power of the Holy Spirit.

Do you know the Holy Spirit will live in you when you believe? This great gift is given to you because of your faith. Take hold of your gift and keep the fire burning in your heart. This fire that has started will spread and bring your heart close to Jesus. You will never have to wonder if Jesus loves you, and you will never have to ask how much because He is faithful to show you.

Those who wait for Jesus will mount up with wings like eagles and soar high. They will run and not be weary and walk and not be faint. Be one who believes and waits upon Jesus so you can rise with power from on high.

# May 5

*"According to your faith be it done to you."*
*Matthew 9:29*

Faith brings us closer to Jesus. By our faith we will believe in things that once were hidden but now are close to our hearts. Our faith will open the door for these things to be revealed and restored. When we let Jesus show us by faith, we will receive clarity and be able to believe without sight.

Have you asked Jesus, believing He will say yes to what you are hoping to receive? Or are you just going through the motions and really do not believe? Ask yourself if you really have faith without seeing all the details and then pray for God to show you His answers to the prayers you are praying.

Jesus promises to show you great and mighty things that you have not yet known. He will give you real answers to your real questions. He never lets you down but will keep on showing you how to grow more faith. He will do what He says He will do, so keep asking, so that according to your faith, it will be done to you.

# May 6

*"Do not fear, only believe."*
**Mark 5:36**

Fear hides in the depths of our weary souls. When we are tired, we stop pushing through to let Jesus solve the problem. Unfortunately, we let it defeat us. The surmounting issues become mountains we cannot move. How about raising the faith flag high over fear so that our faith will rise to new heights? If we do, our fear will vanish, and our faith will bring victory through Jesus Christ.

Fear is a liar and will stop you in your tracks. Fear keeps you from doing what God really wants you to do. Fear tells you to stop counting on the wonder-working power of Jesus because your mind focuses on what you think can't happen instead of what can happen through faith in Jesus Christ. Will you choose fear or faith?

Do you find yourself bringing fear with you wherever you go? Maybe you want to stop being afraid, but your heart keeps worrying about what you cannot change. Choose to believe, and fear will stop interrupting your thoughts. Pray for your heart to turn to Jesus and believe so fear will leave.

# May 7

*"The kingdom of God is not coming in ways that
can be observed."*
**Luke 17:20**

The kingdom of God will be revealed in ways that only the Father knows. We must be ready for He will come when it is time. There is a time for everything and a season for all things. We may not see at first, but the promise will be revealed in due time. We might not understand, but God will show us what He has planned in His time.

Do not let your hearts be troubled. Believe all things will work out at the right time. Know that God will bring you through it if He takes you to it. Trust Him and let Him show you what He has for you. Keep sharing the hope that you have so others may believe, too. God wants all to have the saving faith that He brings.

Give the blessings you have received to others so they may see God working in you. Shine His light so they may give thanks to God for what is happening in their lives. They will see that the former things have come to pass and that the new things have come to life. All things are possible to the one who believes and walks with God.

# May 8

*"Not everyone who says to me, 'Lord, Lord,' will enter the kingdom of heaven, but the one who does the will of my Father who is in heaven."*
*Matthew 7:21*

Some will not enter the kingdom of heaven because they did not do the will of the Father. They will not understand why they are outside of the kingdom, but it will be because of their choices. God will reward those who did choose to follow His will. He blesses those who are faithful servants with entrance into the kingdom.

Where can you serve and how can you do the Father's will? Ask Him and listen for His response to you. He will show you where He needs you to shine for His glory. He is looking far and wide for those who will put their feet to faith and go where they are called.

What is the Father calling you to do? Listen to His voice and run to the Father. He wants you to fall into grace so He can pick you up and place you in the perfect place where He will give you instruction. He knows where you can be used to make a difference for His kingdom, so listen and go where He calls you.

# May 9

*"Who touched me?"*
**Mark 5:31**

Jesus knows when people touch Him with their prayers. He offers health and wholeness to those who reach out to Him. There is powerful healing in the hand of the Savior. We all need the touch of Jesus on our lives because He is our Healer.

Do you need a touch from Jesus? Reach for Him, and do not be afraid to ask Him for what your heart desires. He knows your heart and cares for you deeply. In fact, He has been waiting for you to come to Him with your requests so that He can bring you joy.

Joy is found where Jesus is. Call upon Him so He can give you the joy you are seeking. He is always waiting for you, so seek Him while He is close to you. He is near to all who call on Him in truth, so touch Him. Come just as you are and find rest for your soul with Jesus.

# May 10

*"Where have you laid him?"*
*John 11:34*

We all have questions for our Savior. He will take our requests to the Father and give us answers in His timing. But He needs us to listen when He disciplines and directs us in a certain way. He does all for the glory of the Father and prays for us to have a willing heart even if we do not understand.

Jesus knows how you need His loving direction and His kindness. He prays you will not waste time worrying but will make time to see the hope a relationship with Him brings. He is your living hope and is the answer to all your questions.

Pray that you will stop trying to understand everything but will trust Jesus with everything. He has your best interest at heart. Even when questions arise, know that Jesus is on your side. Pray you will let Him direct your heart to His perfect answers. He will never let you down.

# May 11

*"It is not for you to know times or seasons that the Father has fixed by his own authority."*
*Acts 1:7*

We want to know why things happen the way they do. We eagerly await answers to our questions. But the Father will act by His own authority in the way that He wills for us. We must keep seeking Him and listen for His personal instructions as we wait.

Do you hear the Father calling you? He wants you to trust Him without knowing all the details and follow Him without knowing all the answers. He is close to you as you wait upon Him. He is attending to the voice of your prayers.

What is on your heart? Pray with purpose and trust God to give you the desires of your heart. When you do, you will experience the beauty of His plan for you. Only He knows what is best and will give you rest so you can know His will for you. Give Jesus your heart so He can touch yours with His perfect peace.

# May 12

*"Come and you will see."*
*John 1:39*

Our Savior wants us to come to Him so we can fully see Him. He yearns for us to rely on Him so He can help us stay strong. He gets the glory as we turn to Him and let go of our worries and fears that hold us back. His name will be lifted high as we fall on our knees in prayers of thanksgiving.

If your heart is heavy, let Jesus take the weight of your burdens. He knows just how much you love Him and will give you all that you need. Jesus blesses you when you make Him Lord of your life.

Are you ready to see Jesus make a difference in your life? He is the perfecter of your faith and the author of your life. Come just as you are so He can do something new in you. He will change you from the inside out and light your way to the Father who will put His bright light in you. Believe, and He will shine in you!

# May 13

*"Let us go on to the next towns, that I may preach there also, for that is why I came out."*
*Mark 1:38*

Keep speaking about how much Jesus loves. Tell all about the saving grace of Jesus that is available to everyone who believes in Him. There are many who still need to hear the good news about the power of His love and grace. He has come to save us all. Keep speaking and do not be silent, for He wants all to believe!

To whom can you share the hope that is found in Jesus? God will place people in your life who will ask you about the joy that is in you. Be ready to speak about the promises He has given you and the peace He has placed within you. There are more people who need a touch from the Savior so they can be free.

Jesus came so that He could help save us from our sins. He gives so that we can keep going. The world takes, but Jesus gives. Seek Him always, so that He can speak life into you eternally. Do not be hesitant to let others see the hope that has flooded your soul!

# May 14

*"Follow me."*
**Matthew 9:9**

We are all called to follow Jesus. He wants us all to have a relationship with Him so we can follow Him. He gets our full attention when we make Him first in our life. Jesus wants the very best for His children. He gives in abundance so that we can grow tender hearts and generously give to others as He gives to us.

Is Jesus first in your life? Pray you will remove any distractions to make room for Him to live abundantly in you. Clean the inner room of your heart by cleansing your mind of the assumptions that are not true about what Jesus can do. Seek the things that are above where Jesus reigns!

It is in the inner sanctuary of your heart where you will find your home with Jesus. Keep Him close and you will find yourself wanting more time with Him. Jesus speaks when you follow Him. Listen with your heart so He can comfort your soul like no one else can.

# May 15

*"If a kingdom is divided against itself,*
*that kingdom cannot stand."*
**Mark 3:24**

We must be united to stand strong. If we remain divided, we will fall. Jesus wants us to be close to Him by standing together in truth. The way to please Him is to keep working for the common good of all. If we put aside our differences and embrace kindness, we will surely be able to see the victory.

Are you wanting to see unity in your community? There are ways to make a difference for the betterment of all. First, keep your feet firmly planted with Jesus as your foundation and you will be ready to withstand any challenge. He will help you overcome what comes your way.

Then, listen to His commands and obey them. He blesses you when you show your love for Him through an obedient and grateful heart. Seek Him with all your heart and He will awaken you to a new spirit-filled life where you will want to serve others and make a difference for the glory of God.

# May 16

*"You blind Pharisee! First clean the inside of the cup and the plate, that the outside may be clean."*
*Matthew 23:26*

We can be blinded by lies when we take our eyes off Jesus and instead, focus on the world and its ways. But when we clean ourselves from the inside out, we will be refreshed and ready to run our race with eyes fixed on Jesus, the Perfecter of our faith. He protects us when we stay close to Him.

Have you rediscovered your potential as you claim Jesus as your Protector? When you place your trust in Him, He will hold you in the palm of His hands. Never doubt that Jesus will help you. He is strong when you are weak. He covers you with His grace when you give Him your heart.

What areas of your life can you place your trust in Him more? Have you considered that He is waiting on you to make the first move closer to Him? Pray for new eyes to see what Jesus needs you to see so you can come clean. With Him, you will be restored with new vision.

# May 17

*"If anyone would come after me, let him deny himself and take up his cross and follow me."*
*Mark 8:34*

We are all called to be a disciple of Jesus and to make disciples by using our speaking and serving gifts. People need Jesus so they can see the light. We can be examples in this dark world by denying *our* will and following *His* will. There are many who are still walking in lies and need us to speak the truth and serve with kindness.

Are you showing love to those who God puts in your path? Love covers a multitude of sins and blesses all who live in love. Try putting on love and forgive those who have hurt you. Jesus will help you see them with His eyes full of compassion and love when you follow Him.

Where do you need to surrender self to see more of Jesus? Take time today and pray you will let go of all bitterness and offense toward others so that the Holy Spirit will be actively working in you. Forgive as Jesus has forgiven you, and love as Jesus loves you. He is waiting to lift you up with wings like eagles so that you can soar high!

# May 18

*"Blessed are the pure in heart,
for they shall see God."*
*Matthew 5:8*

Those who are close to God will receive His righteousness. He blesses us when we are seeking Him with our whole hearts and turning to Him with all that is within us. He searches far and wide for those whose hearts are turned toward Him. He knows who will stand firm for Him when the fiery trial comes.

Are you shrinking back or drawing closer to God? Think about your priorities. If God is first in your life, He will rule in you. If He is not, then other things are more important, and they will take over your thoughts and desires. When you delight in Him, He will give you the desires of your heart and you will find contentment and peace.

Where is your heart? You will see God if you stay pure in heart and do not let the world steal you away into its temptations and insecurities. Only Jesus can bring you to a right relationship with the Father. Speak His name and invite Him into your life. He wants to make His home in your heart, once and for all!

# *May 19*

> *"Everyone then who hears these words of mine and does them will be like a wise man who built his house on the rock."*
> *Matthew 7:24*

Obedience is the key to a purpose-driven life. We will be closer to God when we hear His words of wisdom and obey them. Trusting God will give us the ability to stand firm even in the face of danger. Fear leaves when God has the center stage in our lives.

Do you hear God calling you to lean on Him for all you need? He is giving you wisdom from above that will allow you to know how to live with purpose. Be still and know that He is God. His words will enlighten you when you make the choice to trust and obey Him.

Listen to His voice in the stillness of your soul. He speaks truth so you will have the blueprints to build your house on the rock. Read His Word that outlines His will for your life. He always gives you hope when you make room for Him.

# May 20

*"Put out into the deep and let down your nets for a catch."*
*Luke 5:4*

There is abundance with Jesus. He loves to bless His children with more than we can ever dream or imagine. He gives bountifully and loves steadfastly. He directs us to places where He can show us His glory. Only those who believe will truly see what He is doing.

Have you asked Jesus to show you where you need to fish for men? He will give you opportunities to share and shine when you follow the light. Look in the places where He directs you. You will see the light of His love shining the brightest where there are the deepest needs.

Put your net into the deep waters. There you will find opportunities like never before. The quantity of people that need Jesus will overwhelm you. But Jesus will empower you with the Holy Spirit who will give you courage and strength to fight the good fight of the faith.

# May 21

*"I, Jesus, have sent my angel to testify to you about these things for the churches. I am the root and descendant of David, the bright morning star."*
*Revelation 22:16*

Jesus shines as the bright morning star in our hearts when He is the love of our life. He wants us to come to Him with our whole hearts so He can save us. He is our Savior who descended from David to save us all. He hopes we will come to believe so that we can be saved.

Come as you are into His marvelous light. Let His face shine down on you and give you peace. There is no place for worry or fear where Jesus reigns. The Messiah has come to save and seek you so yoke yourself to Him.

Are you letting His light shine in you? He is calling you to come closer to His love. If you look to Him, you will have His light in you as bright as the beautiful morning star. His light cannot be extinguished, so let your light shine!

# May 22

*"You therefore must be perfect,
as your heavenly Father is perfect."*
*Matthew 5:48*

We have the opportunity to make the best decisions when we listen to the Father and obey Him. He speaks truth to us for our good and His glory. Those who are close to the Father aim to please Him and will seek His perfect will in His timing.

Are you seeking God's will for you? He wants you to be ready in and out of season to listen to Him and obey His truth. He will point you to the best decision and give you courage to take the next step. Choose the perfect way through the direction of the Holy Spirit.

Make a commitment to choose joy at all times and never lose sight of why God put you where you are for such a time as this. Your yes will open the door for richer blessings. Remember it is far better to give than to receive. Just do it!

# May 23

*"Therefore pray earnestly to the Lord of the harvest*
*to send out laborers into his harvest."*
**Matthew 9:38**

God needs more laborers to work diligently for His kingdom. He asks that we pray for these workers to join Him in the work that He is already doing. He needs all of us to be co-laborers working together in unity with His power from above.

Have you prayed for more laborers? God hears your prayers and will answer you when you lift your requests to Him. He needs people to make a difference, and you are one of His chosen. Keep your heart close to Him and your mind focused on His plans for you.

Every day is another opportunity for you to work diligently and passionately. The fields are ripe for harvesting for new believers and God is looking for you to labor with Him to find them. With His power working in you, more work can be done for His kingdom. Get ready, get set, and go!

# May 24

*"Peace to you!"*
*Luke 24:36*

God brings peace to us in all situations. When we focus on His peace and remain in His presence, we will feel His perfect peace. Peace is possible with God, and God alone will bring us out of the stress and the mess.

Are you feeling burdened by your current situation? God is offering you peace beyond human understanding. He feels your pain and yearns to take all your cares and concerns. Peace is not the absence of problems, but the presence of Christ.

Pray that you will find peace with Christ and not be pressured by the issues before you. He can do what no one else can do. He will give you peace to stand strong under pressure. Believe and receive peace from your Lord and Savior.

# May 25

*"John baptized with water,*
*but you will be baptized with the Holy Spirit."*
**Acts 11:16**

Repent, for the kingdom of heaven is at hand. Jesus wants us to turn toward Him and believe. He baptizes with the Holy Spirit when we believe and put our trust in Him. The Holy Spirit will invade our hearts and minds when Jesus is our Lord.

Have you put your full faith and trust in Jesus? If so, you have the Holy Spirit living inside of you. He will help you make the decisions that are before you. He will teach you all things if you will be still and listen. He will defend you when you sit in silence and let Him fight your battles.

Jesus wants to be your Lord. He yearns for you to come close to Him so that He can lift you higher than your problems. No issue is too difficult for Him to work out. Believe that nothing is impossible for your Lord because He *can* move your mountain. The kingdom of heaven is at hand!

# May 26

*"See, you are well! Sin no more,*
*that nothing worse may happen to you."*
*John 5:14*

**D**o we believe we can be made well? Jesus tells us to sin no more so that we can find hope and move forward again. He gives us courage to step out of the darkness and into the light of His love where joy resides.

Pray for the strength to keep going with Jesus by your side. He sees your struggle and will take your burdens. It is your choice about how you will live your life. He hopes you will choose Him.

Remember every day is a gift from Jesus. Ask Him to show you where you can take His message of love to a hurting world and then go make disciples. You will see that you are well when you share like Jesus. He will take away your worries and replace them with peace.

# May 27

**"I who speak to you am he."**
**John 4:26**

Jesus speaks to us. He is the way, the truth, and the life, and our Messiah who came to set us free. He wants to change our lives by making His home in us. He knows us very well and loves every part of us.

Do you hear Him speaking to you? Open your Bible and hear His words that will touch your heart. He knows you by name and has written it in the palm of His hand. This truth will encourage your soul and bring you closer to Him.

Turn to the Prince of Peace, Jesus Christ. He brings peace to all who are His. He wants to take your hand in His and bring you to the other side with Him. Let Him reign in your heart and soul to experience perfect peace that remains.

# May 28

*"Is it lawful to heal on the Sabbath, or not?"*
**Luke 14:3**

God gives us a Sabbath for our health and our rest. He wants us to rest in Him. But when we need healing, He will surely heal even if it is on the Sabbath. We will hear Him when He calls our name. We will be made whole when we surrender control and let Him revive us.

Where do you need healing? Call upon Jesus and He will attend to the voice of your prayers. He will revive your heart when you make Him Lord of your life. Put Him in your reach and He will touch your heart with His healing hand.

You have a friend in Jesus. He needs you to stop chasing lies because the truth lies in Him. Remember He brings blessings to those who put Him first. Where is Jesus in your life? Make the choice today to put Him in first place so you will experience all He has to offer you.

# *May 29*

*"For whoever does the will of God,*
*he is my brother and sister and mother."*
*Mark 3:35*

God has chosen us to do His will. Jesus calls us brothers and sisters when we do what God's will is for us. He looks favorably to those who put aside self to serve Him. He needs all of us to do our part for the kingdom of God.

Where can you serve? If you do not know where you are needed, pray constantly, and ask God to show you. He will open doors as you seek to serve Him. Kindness flows when God is honored, and relationships are respected.

God is listening to your prayers and answering your requests so His will can be done. He can use you when you trust Him with all your heart and lean not on your own understanding. Your path will be straight when you acknowledge Him in all your ways. Where is God taking you? Obey His promptings and step out of your comfort zone.

# May 30

*"But what comes out of the mouth proceeds from the heart, and this defiles a person."*
*Matthew 15:18*

We can say things that hurt others when we are not walking close to God. Our mouth can get us in trouble if we do not listen to the Spirit of the Lord before we speak. Our hearts can be far from God when we put ourselves above Him. But God will help us do what is right when we make sure we are living close to Him.

Have you said something hurtful to someone recently? Take time to ask God for forgiveness and seek to make things right with that person if possible. Be a peacemaker and bring peace wherever you go. Blessed are you, when you are a peacemaker, for you shall be called a child of God.

God sees you and approves of what you are trying to do. He knows why you said those things and He forgives you. He loves to see all His children getting along together and will reward those who seek His Kingdom and righteousness first. Seek God and you will live!

# May 31

*"Blessed rather are those who hear the word of God and keep it!"*
*Luke 11:28*

We are blessed when we hear the word of God and strive to keep it. God knows how much we love Him by how we trust and obey His commands. He manifests Himself to those who listen and follow what He says. His word blesses us as we live it out.

Keep seeking to know Him and you will see Him working all things for good. He knows what you need even before you do and will open doors for you as you ask, seek, and knock. He listens to you and gives in abundance,

Are you listening to His word and keeping His commandments? You will be blessed when you do both. It is imperative that you listen and obey as you seek the Lord. If you know what to do and do not do it, you will miss the blessings He has for you. Seek to do what He has for you. There are blessings waiting just for you!

# I AM
## THE WAY, THE TRUTH, AND THE LIFE.
### *No one comes to the Father*
### except through Me.

JOHN 14:6

# June 1

*"Neither will I tell you by what authority I do
these things."*
***Luke 20:8***

Jesus wants us to trust Him without having to know all the details. If you truly love Him with all your heart and seek to do His will, He will speak truth and life into you. Jesus has authority given to Him by God for His glory. When we just trust and surrender all to Him, He will show us the right way.

Are you looking for the way? Jesus is the way, the truth, and the life. Come to Him and you will find all you need. Only Jesus can bring light to the darkness and complete healing to the brokenhearted. He knows how much you need Him.

What do you need to confess to Jesus? He is waiting with open arms to help you. He is always listening, and He knows how much you need Him. He will never leave you. Trust Him and you will clearly see the Way!

# June 2

*"But those that were sown on the good soil are the ones who hear the word and accept it and bear fruit, thirtyfold and sixtyfold and a hundredfold."*
*Mark 4:20*

Our faith will grow in good soil if we receive the word with hearts close to Jesus. We can receive His word, and believe, because we are abiding in Him and know the truth. As we abide, we will bear much fruit for His kingdom.

Do you hear the word and accept it because you are abiding in Jesus? Listen to Him calling you into a closer relationship with Him. Look to Him with eagerness and hope because He calls you friend. He has so much to tell you, so listen carefully.

No one comes to the Father except through Jesus. Do you believe? He will rescue you with His grace when you say Yes to Him and seek to know Him. Joy will flood your soul, and you will be made new in Him. Those who come to Christ will receive the word with hope and enter into His kingdom of grace upon grace.

# June 3

*"See that no one knows about it."*
**Matthew 9:30**

Jesus asks us to listen to what He tells us. He has particular instructions for each of us. When He speaks, we must listen. When He instructs, we must obey. We cannot ignore the still small voice from the Holy Spirit. If we do, we will miss what is expected of us.

Jesus heals you mentally, spiritually, and physically for your good and His glory. He will help you when you ask, seek, and knock. He loves to answer the prayers of His children and knows exactly how you need His caring touch upon you. Come to Jesus who will offer all that you need.

What do you need? Ask the Healer who is greater than the healing and He will attend to the voice of your prayers. He comes with healing in His wings just for you at His chosen time. There is no place for worry when Jesus is in control. Yoke yourself to Jesus and let the chains holding you captive fall away.

# June 4

*"Come out of the man, you unclean spirit!"*
*Mark 5:8*

Jesus commands evil to leave. There is no room for darkness in the place where Jesus reigns. His presence makes the enemy shutter and run. The unclean become clean with Jesus Christ when we let Him cleanse us from our sins.

What sin is holding you back from a closer relationship with Jesus? Pray that you can surrender all to Him and repent. He will take all and release the hold the enemy has upon you. Make the choice to turn back to Jesus and be free again.

Sin will not win when Jesus is first in your life. What can you release to Him so that He can take it from you? Release it and give it all to Jesus. He is the Redeemer of your Life and the Overseer of your soul.

# June 5

*"And behold, I am sending the promise of my Father upon you. But stay in the city until you are clothed with power from on high."*
*Luke 24:49*

The Father sends us a promise of power from the Holy Spirit for all who believe. He wants us to surrender to Him and put our trust completely in Him. When we say yes, He will clothe us with power from on high.

Have you surrendered all to Jesus? He is waiting to give you the promised gift of the Holy Spirit. Only Jesus can give you this glorious gift. Wait for Him so He can restore you to Himself like only He can do.

Stay close and you will be covered. Keep Jesus first and you will be safe. Let go of what is holding you down and you will be free once again. As you surrender, freedom from fear and worry will flow from the Spirit. Pray to hold on to hope and remember there is power in the name of Jesus.

# June 6

*"I have said all these things to you to keep you from*
*falling away."*
*John 16:1*

We need to listen to Jesus and obey His commands for us so that we will not fall away and fall into trouble. He instructs us so that we can keep our eyes on Him. The difference between fear and faith is focus. Make every effort to remain focused on Jesus.

Is Jesus the center of your life and your focus? If He is, you will find that His commands will not be burdensome but will be essential to the growth of your faith. Not only will He guide you on the right path, but He will give you strength and endurance to fight to the end and finish your race.

Think about the ways Jesus has given you hope in the past. Write these blessings on your heart and mind and then thank Him for all that He has done for you. Pray for His will to be done in your life as you strive to stay the course with Him no matter what comes your way.

# June 7

*"I am the way, and the truth, and the life. No one comes to the Father except through me."*
*John 14:6*

Jesus is the only way to the Father. When we believe in Him and give our hearts to Him, we are granted access to His Father above. We can have a relationship with Him when we make our home with Him. He is the only way, and the solid rock of truth, and the secret to a joy-filled life.

Do you want more joy? There is joy in your journey when you journey with Jesus and make Him the center of your life. He brings light to the darkness and hope to the hopeless. Do not fret about what has not happened but be grateful for what is to come as you continue to pray.

Jesus is calling you into relationship with Him. He sees you and loves you. He has been waiting to take your burdens from you for some time now. Let them go and yoke up to Jesus Christ. He will fill you with joy and hope!

# June 8

*"What you are going to do, do quickly."*
*John 13:27*

We see bad things happening all around us and we just feel helpless and hopeless. But we have a Savior who has carried all our sins to help us and give us hope. Jesus knew what it was like to have people coming against Him. He would be arrested and suffer unto death to save us from our sins. But death did not win because He was resurrected to give us new life in Him.

Do you feel mistreated or misunderstood? Know that Jesus will rescue you from whatever you are facing so that you can rise above it all. He makes all things new and that includes you.

Tell Jesus how much you need Him and He will attend to the voice of your prayers. He brings good out of all those things that are bringing you down. Those problems have no control over you when you speak Jesus over every situation.

# June 9

*"See my hands and my feet, that it is I myself.*
*Touch me, and see. For a spirit does not have flesh*
*and bones as you see that I have."*
*Luke 24:39*

Jesus wants us to touch and see Him. He lives so that we may have life and have it abundantly. His Spirit lives in us so we can walk with power and strength looking always to Him for all we need. He continues to provide for us as we grow in grace and love.

Where do you need to see Jesus at work in you? Ask Him to show you how you can be used for His glory and go be that light of love. There are many who need to be touched by His love to see.

Jesus saves and sets the captives free. Open the door to your heart and let His marvelous light in. Jesus shines in those who invite Him in their lives. Where will you shine His light today?

# June 10

*"And if he sins against you seven times in the day, and turns to you seven times saying, 'I repent,' you must forgive him."*
*Luke 17:4*

Forgiveness is commanded by Jesus. He gives us many opportunities to forgive others as He has forgiven us. When we forgive, we are following the commands of Jesus. There are many who need our forgiveness and grace.

Has someone hurt you? Jesus sees your broken heart and is near to you. He will hold you up and give you courage to accept apologies and repentance from the offender. He blesses those who trust His way. Tell Him what is bothering you and listen to His loving voice counseling you.

Who will you stretch your hand out to forgive? Jesus is watching your actions and hoping you will make forgiveness and grace part of your story. It is easier to forgive than to hold on to offense and bitterness. Discover that forgiveness sets you free, indeed!

# June 11

*"Therefore do not be anxious about tomorrow, for tomorrow will be anxious for itself. Sufficient for the day is its own trouble."*
*Matthew 6:34*

We can be anxious about tomorrow or we can choose to trust Jesus more today. Jesus wants us to stay calm knowing that He will take care of us. He is our source of strength and our hope for tomorrow. Anxiety leaves when our trust rises.

Where do you need to trust Jesus more? He wants you to lean on Him and not your own understanding. He gives you peace over your problems even in the storm. That cloud will leave as you let the rainbow of Jesus's love shine over you.

Pray that you will let all your burdens go instead of holding onto them. The world and its worries are not too big for Jesus. The world has not seen the magnitude of what Jesus can do. He is bigger than any problem you will ever face!

# June 12

*"As the living Father sent me, and I live because of the Father, so whoever feeds on me, he also will live because of me."*
*John 6:57*

When we feed on Jesus and His words of truth, we will live. The Father sent Him to us so that we could live with peace and be free from the weight of sin. He knew that we needed a Savior to set us free from the sins that try to tear us down, so He gave us Jesus. What a glorious reminder of His eternal love and grace!

Have you made Jesus your Lord and Savior? He has come for you and wants you to make your home with Him. Why do you think He died and rose again? He did it all so you could live! Remember Jesus loves you so much no matter what your past looks like.

Repent and turn toward Jesus. It is time to look up at Him instead of hanging your head down in shame and regret. With Jesus, there is only hope and freedom. Nothing can separate you from His love. Thank Jesus for His everlasting love for you and feed on His promises right now.

# June 13

*"A little while, and you will see me no longer; and
again a little while, and you will see me."*
**John 16:16**

Jesus promised His disciples that they would
see Him again even after He had to go to the
Father. They did not want Him to leave them,
but He promised that it would be better for them if He
went because He could live in them and not just
beside them.

Jesus inside you is better than Jesus beside you. Have
you wondered why that is true? Jesus will give you
the gift of the power and presence of the Holy Spirit
to live inside you as you believe in Him. He will
guide you to all truth and teach you all things. He will
be with you every moment of your life when you
choose to believe.

You will see Jesus in all that you do when He is Lord
of your life. Do you need to be comforted and
encouraged right now? Close your eyes and surrender
all to Jesus who will give you the Holy Spirit to be
with you always. You will see Him if you choose to
believe. He will never leave you!

# June 14

*"Cast the net on the right side of the boat,
and you will find some."*
**John 21:6**

The disciples of Jesus needed His guidance and direction in many ways and in all things they encountered. They saw miracles and witnessed new life. They saw tears turn to joy and discovered that their faith would grow as they leaned on Jesus and not their own understanding.

Jesus will help you see even in the mundane tasks of life. He will point you to the answer if you call upon Him in spirit and in truth. He will show you the best way to live when you seek His kingdom and all His righteousness above all things.

Your net will be full when Jesus is in the boat with you. He will show you where to cast your hope when you trust Him and cling to His promises. Where do you need to see the promises of Jesus fulfilled in your net of life? Ask in the name of Jesus so that His will may be done in your life, now and forevermore.

# June 15

*"These things I have spoken to you while I am still with you."*
*John 14:25*

Jesus speaks to us and waits for us to respond. He has much to tell us and will strengthen our soul when we seek Him with all our hearts. His commandments are for our good and not for our harm. Everything He shares will give us new encouragement for the road ahead because our race is not finished.

Fix your eyes upon Jesus and gaze at His wonderful face while you run your race. He rewards you with power to keep going as you keep on the straight and narrow path with Him. Only Jesus can give you the extra endurance you need to finish strong.

Are you listening with your heart? Jesus will lift you up with His lessons of love. He is the living hope who came to help solve your problems and turn away from sin. Because He lives, you can live freely. Since the Son has set you free, you are free, indeed!

# June 16

*"I am the bread of life; whoever comes to me shall not hunger, and whoever believes in me shall never thirst."*
**John 6:35**

Jesus is the bread of life who has come to feed us with food that will bring us life everlasting. He wants to give us living water so that we will never be thirsty again. He promises that whoever lives with Him will be renewed by His spiritual strength and everyone who believes will be saved.

Have you surrendered all to Jesus? Jesus will give you new life when you give Him *all* your heart. He wants the whole portion and not just a part of it. He will speak love over you as you let go of control and let Him fill you with His food and water.

Is there an empty place that you are trying to fill with temporary things? Instead of those things, fill yourself with heavenly things that come in your life when you seek first the kingdom of God and all His righteousness. His food will strengthen your body and refresh your soul.

# June 17

We will hold fast to the traditions of men over the commandments of God when we keep our focus on being seen by the world instead of being seen by God. Man has an outward focus, whereas God looks on the inside at our heart. He knows every hair on our head and every thought in our mind. He made us out of love to love.

He speaks love over you and wants you to love Him with all your heart, mind, and soul. This is the greatest commandment that needs to be obeyed to have a deeper relationship with Him. Deep calls to deep at the sound of His beautiful voice speaking truth to you. Do you hear Him? Will you obey Him?

You can build new faith by making Jesus your foundation instead of man-made traditions. He commands you live out what He speaks in word and in deed. Put to memory the greatest commandment to love Him with all your heart, soul, and mind and then do it!

# June 18

*"But to what shall I compare this generation? It is like children sitting in the marketplaces and calling to their playmates."*
*Matthew 11:16*

This generation seeks to be seen by friends and noticed for what they have. God wants us to stop comparing ourselves with others to the point where we become insecure and jealous. Extreme competition can ruin a relationship when God is not honored or respected. He wants us to listen to what He says instead of worrying about what others say.

Are you listening to God speak truth to you? He wants you to put His teachings above all others so He can open your heart to hear. God is faithful even when others are not. He will raise you up when you step out of your comfort zone with Him.

Your friends might not step out with you, but God will always be with you. He needs you to stand firm and keep obeying even when it is hard and when you do not understand. He rewards those who put Him first and make every effort to supplement faith with works from God. You have an assignment tailor-made from God. Come and see what it is!

# June 19

*"One who is faithful in a very little is also faithful in much, and one who is dishonest in a very little is also dishonest in much."*
*Luke 16:10*

Faithfulness brings plentiful peace and abounding hope. Jesus wants to see us faithful in all that we do. He wants us to believe. Those who remain faithful in the little things will have great faith in the bigger things. But those who are dishonest even in the little things, will be dishonest in big ways.

Will you stay faithful no matter what comes your way? Jesus speaks hope over you when you keep believing for what you hope for even before it happens. Keep praying in faith and Jesus will be honored by your prayers and give you more than you can ever dream or imagine.

He will also saturate you in His glory when you keep Him first place in your heart. His glory reigns in those who let Him reign in them. That person who is trying to steal your joy will not win when Jesus is center of your life. Keep your eyes upon Jesus and your joy will be full!

# June 20

*"If anyone loves me, he will keep my word, and my Father will love him, and we will come to him and make our home with him."*
*John 14:23*

The Father loved us so much that He gave us His Son. Jesus came to lift us up out of our shame and asked the Father to forgive us. He was our light, when the darkness tried to overcome us. He was our rock, when we felt the weight of our sin crashing down on us. He was our hope, when we thought we could not make it another day.

You prayed, and He listened. You hoped, and He showed you what only He could do. You cried, and He caught your tears in His bottle. You laughed, and He smiled. You asked for peace, and He gave you His gift of the Holy Spirit. You wanted joy, and He made room in your heart for Him. You obeyed, and He saw how much you loved Him.

You have everything when Jesus is Lord and Savior of your life. He will infuse you with strength, grant you peace, and heal your weary soul. He will comfort you when you are brokenhearted. What do you need right now? Ask and receive His will for you.

# June 21

*"I tell you, if these were silent,*
*the very stones would cry out."*
**Luke 19:40**

J esus is so powerful that even if the truth about
Him is suppressed, the rocks would cry out about
how great He is! Nothing can stop the truth about
Him from being told. His power and might are
incomprehensible and unstoppable. Nothing is too
hard for Jesus to overcome. He is bigger than
anything we will ever face.

Who is trying to hinder your testimony of faith?
Instead of worrying about how you could offend
someone, try sharing your story with as many people
as you can. Tell how Jesus has changed your heart
and stretched your faith. Give examples of how He
has made a difference in your life.

Jesus needs you to reach people with His love. He
wants you to talk about the hope that is in you
because you have a relationship with Him. His
kingdom message is for all. Be a difference maker
who encourages others to put their full faith and trust
in Him. You will never regret standing up for Jesus
Christ!

# June 22

*"The kingdom of heaven is like treasure hidden in a field, which a man found and covered up. Then in his joy he goes and sells all that he has and buys that field."*
*Matthew 13:44*

The kingdom of heaven is for all who treasure Jesus and put their full faith and trust in Him. When we look to Jesus as our Savior, He gives us more than we can ask or imagine just because He loves us so much. Look at His joyful face and see that His amazing grace is more than enough.

Jesus wants you to seek Him with all your heart so your joy will be full. He yearns to give you the desires of your heart. He asks that you make room for Him in the depths of your soul so He can show you how much He loves you. There is no stopping Him, so keep Him close at all times.

What battle are you facing? Take Jesus with you and you will be victorious. Remember how He fought the battle for you before and know He will do it again! You need only to be still and to trust Him. Pray for courage and watch what Jesus does! You will be overwhelmed by how Jesus works all things out for good!

# June 23

***"By your endurance you will gain your lives."***
***Luke 21:19***

We have heard that when the going gets tough, the tough gets going. Jesus adds that by our endurance we will gain our lives. We must endure some things in this life. At times, the grind gets to us, and it is tougher than we can ever imagine. Life is hard and we must cling to our Savior to give us perseverance in this ever-changing world. We can do all things with Jesus who strengthens us.

What challenge are you facing right now? Jesus will help you endure this situation until it is solved or dissolved. He does not want you to be weary or worried. He sees the health issues you are facing, and He can heal you. He knows how much you are struggling to make ends meet and He can provide for you.

Trust Jesus and give Him control over all these things so He can make all things new for you. He restores you to Himself and brings healing in His wings. Greater things are possible for you if you believe that you will receive in His will and timing. Pray for more faith to rise up in you!

# June 24

*"When the Spirit of truth comes, he will guide you into all the truth, for he will not speak on his own authority, but whatever he hears he will speak, and he will declare to you the things that are to come."*
**John 16:13**

The Spirit of truth has come to bring truth to all. He guides us into all truth by speaking declarations over us. He knows how much we need Him, so He came as the truth so that all who believe will have eternal life. Be prepared to listen and speak to others what He teaches right now. He will surely come again, so be ready.

Is fear holding you back from receiving the promises of Jesus? Fear has no place with Jesus by your side. For God has not given us a spirit of fear, but of power, and of love, and of a sound mind. Tune in to the power of love, not the spirit of fear.

Are you listening? The truth is knocking at your door. Open the door and let Him in so that you can personally know the truth and let the truth set you free. No more chains can hold you when Jesus is your Lord. Freedom and truth have a name and that name is Jesus!

# June 25

*"Blessed are the eyes that see what you see!"*
**Luke 10:23**

Jesus blesses us with eyes to see. He opens our eyes when we look to Him and not our self-interests. How wonderful it is to see with spiritual eyes as we gaze at our world! We can see the lost when we look for them. We can see the spiritually blind when we shift our focus outwardly and pray for God to help us see these people.

In the kingdom of God, the last will be the first and the first will be the last. What Jesus wants is for you to put your own interests aside to help those who are struggling and conflicted. Is there someone you can help right now? Pray for eyes to see those who need Jesus and bless them with His love.

Do you see what Jesus wants you to see? He is helping you see what really matters. He is showing you who needs your help. He will bring you to those you can serve. Leaders in His kingdom serve others. Ask Jesus to show you where you can help Him and go be a servant where He calls you.

# June 26

*"Come to me, all who labor and are heavy laden, and I will give you rest."*
*Matthew 11:28*

Jesus promises us rest. He knows we are weary and heavy-laden with all that we have before us. He even knows our bodies weaken from all the work we must do. He asks us to come to Him so He can give us the rest we need to keep going. What a wonderful Savior we have in Jesus who provides restoration for our bodies and strength for our souls!

With Jesus as your Savior, He will set your heart on fire so that whatever is bothering you will vanish into thin air. With Jesus as your Redeemer, you will mount up with wings like eagles and run and not be weary. With Jesus as your Lord, You will walk with Him and not faint because He will hold you up. There is life and victory when you come as you are and fall in the arms of Jesus.

Are you needing a break from all the work before you? Close your eyes, breathe in His Spirit, and relax your body and mind. Let it all go and give your burdens to Jesus. He cares for you and wants to rescue you from the stress. Rest in Him.

# June 27

*"And then if anyone says to you, 'Look, here is the Christ!' or 'Look there he is!' do not believe it."*
**Mark 13:21**

Jesus is the way, the truth, and the life. He is the Christ, the Son of the living God, and there is no other. Do not believe others when they falsely name others as the Messiah, for Christ is the only one. There will be others who try to say otherwise, or who do not believe, but do not fall for this. Christ is the only way to the Father.

Do you believe that Jesus loves you? Receive His love and be set free from what is keeping you from fully believing. Christ is the one who will open your heart and settle your soul. He came for you and is waiting for you to choose Him. His love is everlasting, and His grace is overpowering. There is nothing that can keep His love from covering you, except you.

Will you make the choice to let it all go and let Christ fully in your life? Lay it all down and come to the Savior who will truly set you free. His love is abounding and abundant. His grace will save you and give you hope once again. Say Yes to Jesus, once and for all!

HE SPEAKS TO ME

# June 28

*"Foxes have holes, and birds of the air have nests, but the Son of Man has nowhere to lay his head."*
*Matthew 8:20*

Jesus has come to make His home with us. He will chase us until we finally surrender and let Him in our lives. He will never give up on us. He runs after His prodigals, those who have left, with forgiving love because He wants us to come back home. He never leaves us, and He will never give up on us.

Jesus is chasing you. He will go wherever you are to find you and set you free. His love follows you wherever life takes you. You cannot outrun Jesus. He is before, behind, and around you. When you give Him your heart, He will live inside you in the power of the Holy Spirit to be with you always.

How wonderful it is to know that Jesus never leaves! He does not stay in one place as His Spirit lives in you because you believed. Walk with Him, talk with Him, and obey Him. Listen to His love teaching you what to do and where to go. He will help you as you stop trying to control life on your own and start trusting Him more for all you need.

# June 29

*"I am the resurrection and the life. Whoever believes in me, though he die, yet shall he live."*
*John 11:25*

Jesus is the resurrection and the life! Death did not defeat Him. He came to live in us so that we can live. His sacrifice gave us everlasting life that remains with us to eternity. His love remains. How wonderful to know that we can have resurrection power living in us when we believe!

Do you believe? His power lives in you and works in you to overcome all the struggles of this life. Close your eyes and picture Jesus giving you His gift of the Holy Spirit to dwell within you. Unwrap it and hold Him tight. Feel His presence providing new peace. Breathe in His breath of fresh love that will empower you with new strength for the journey ahead.

Faith grows as the Spirit settles in your heart, mind, and your soul and you listen to His promptings. Have you heard what the Spirit is telling you? If so, what are you waiting for? Start now by obeying what He tells you and go do what He needs you to do. He needs you to march on to victory with the resurrection power of Jesus!

# June 30

*"In that day you will ask nothing of me. Truly, truly, I say to you, whatever you ask of the Father in my name, he will give it to you."*
*John 16:23*

We pray and we wait for answers. But are we asking the Father in the name of Jesus as we pray? The Father hears our prayers and will answer in His timing. His answer is either, *yes*, because it is His will or, *no*, because He has something better for us. He answers in His perfect timing knowing our present, past, and our future. Sometimes our prayers will take time to see an answer because He wants us to wait and draw closer to Him to see His glory revealed.

What are you asking of the Father? He wants you to keep praying and asking in the name of Jesus. He hears you. Take time today and pray in the Spirit for the Father to show you His will. He wants to see your faith grow. Pray and stay faithful so that He can see your devotion and determination.

Write down your prayers and then ask the Father for what you need, believing that He can and will help you.

TAKE HEART;
*it is I.*

# DO NOT BE AFRAID.

MARK 6:50

# July 1

*"Why are you making a commotion and weeping?
The child is not dead but sleeping."*
**Mark 5:39**

Jesus heals and brings us back to life. He knows how much we need His healing touch now. His healing is not just for the past, He heals today. Weeping will turn to joy in His kingdom. He will wipe away our tears and take away our fears. Wake up to the joy of Jesus!

Will you turn to Him? He needs to see your faith right now. Jesus will touch you with His healing hands. He makes all things new and that includes you. Ask for spiritual healing and you shall receive more of the joy of Jesus!

Jesus is waiting to see your smile, knowing that He is healing your body right now. He brightens your eyes with light as the eyes are the lamp of the body showing health and wholeness. Believe, before you receive, and the peace of Christ will enrich your heart and comfort your soul. Is it well with your soul?

# July 2

*"Therefore render to Caesar the things that are
Caesar's, and to God the things that are God's."
Matthew 22:21*

Jesus wants us to render to God the things that are
His and to Caesar the things that are Caesar's.
We must respect authority and obey as God
commands. As we obey, we will be rewarded with
His blessings from above. The riches from God far
outweigh any material things. There are blessings that
only He can give us when we give from our heart.

Will you give without complaining? He loves to give
to His children in abundance and hopes to see us give
from our hearts. It is far better to give than to receive.
Live out this command and see how much joy will fill
your heart again. There is joy to be found when you
have the proper perspective.

The giver of the most perfect gift is God, who gave
His Son, so that you could be saved and have eternal
life. Jesus suffered for your sins because He loves
you. He never complained but did what the Father
asked of Him. What is the Father asking you to do?
Seek Him so that you can hear His voice instructing
you and then make every effort to obey His will.

# July 3

*"For I have not spoken on my own authority, but the Father who sent me has himself given me a commandment-what to say and what to speak."*
*John 12:49*

Jesus speaks to us what the Father says to Him. He has been given the commandment about what to say and when to say it. We must listen to His voice instead of questioning what we hear so we can be obedient to do His will. Let us be obedient to do what Jesus says, knowing it is straight from the Father and spoken for our good.

Do you hear His voice speaking truth to you? Do not let the weight of the world hold you down, but let Jesus lift you up. He has come to bring you peace because He has overcome the world. So, take heart and feel His peace covering you like no one else can. His peace will help you get through anything you will ever face!

Tell Jesus what is bothering you. He is listening to your voice and will make a way where there seems to be no way. He brings peace to comfort you and strength to keep you on the right path. Stay with Jesus as you wait for the problems to fade. He will never let you go. What a wonderful friend we have in Jesus!

# July 4

*"Blessed are those who mourn, for they shall be comforted."*
*Matthew 5:4*

Jesus sees our broken hearts and hears our cries. He knows who, and what, we have lost and wants to heal us from the inside out. He will come close to those who need Him when we make the choice to draw closer to Him. Blessed are those who mourn because they will comforted by Jesus Christ who heals with His peace.

Take His hand and let Him lead you to still waters and green pastures. He is there for you wherever you go. He will show you the victory when you trust Him with all that is within you. Give up the fight and try letting it all go. Jesus has promised to take it from you so that He can fight your battles.

These challenges are opportunities to grow closer to Him one day at a time. There are lessons to be learned and choices to grow your faith. He will be there for you in no time. Give it all to Jesus so that He can lift you up with eagle's wings in due time!

# July 5

*"Pay attention to yourselves! If your brother sins, rebuke him, and if he repents, forgive him."*
**Luke 17:3**

We all need forgiveness because we have all sinned and have fallen short of the glory of God. We are all in need of a Savior who will catch us when we fall. Just as we all need forgiveness from Jesus, we all need to extend forgiveness to others if they repent.

Have you paid attention to what Jesus is telling you? He will speak truth to you when you listen to His voice directing you to an action. He knows who has hurt you because it hurts Him, too. He does not like to see His children fighting. Maybe it is time to repent and ask for forgiveness.

Seek to live in the Spirit and the peace of Christ will cover you. Get rid of the bitterness and the grace of Jesus will overshadow the anger in you. Seek more of Jesus and His joy will overpower you. Give more of yourself to serve and His love will overwhelm you. Forgive, and faith will rise up in you!

# July 6

*"It is said, 'You shall not put the Lord your God to the test.'"*
*Luke 4:12*

We shall not put our Lord God to the test. He does not want us to test Him so He can prove things to us, but He wants us to trust and obey Him. He will show us what we need to do if we keep our faith and stay the course with His direction. He is Lord over all, so honor, love, and fear the Lord our God who brings truth to us.

Do you fear the Lord? He is speaking to you and has much love for you. When you fear Him, the Lord will see your faithfulness to Him. He wants to see your love in action as you obey His commandments. Your obedience will bring you closer to His love.

What do you want to say to the Savior who set you free? Instead of asking why things are happening, maybe start thanking Him for all He has done for you because of His great love. His love conquers all. Know this truth and you will be set free from any doubt that might enter your mind.

# July 7

*"Do not grumble among yourselves."*
*John 6:43*

God does not want us to be at odds with each other. He sees the division among us and the quarreling that is taking place around us. He notices the grumbling and complaining and it hurts Him to see us this way. We all can make the choice to be positive and polite even in a world that tries to pull us away from peace.

Will you be a peacemaker even in situations that seem impossible? People need peace and you can be the one person who brings peace wherever you go. Jesus speaks peace over you to spread His peace. Before you step out and start a new day, pray that Jesus will help you bring peace and let go of any offense that is bothering you.

Where does Jesus need you to bring His peace? Think about all the issues in your life that might have conflict in them and focus on how peace would calm these situations. If it depends on you, step out and be the peacemaker with Jesus guiding all your words and actions. You will see Jesus at work where peace is the answer.

# July 8

*"But when the Helper comes, whom I will send to you from the Father, the Spirit of truth, who proceeds from the Father, he will bear witness about me."*
**John 15:26**

Jesus has given us a Helper from the Father. He is the Spirit of truth who will show us all things and bear witness about Jesus. This Helper, the Holy Spirit, will dwell within us when we make Jesus our Lord and Savior. He is with us as we surrender to His leading and make the choice to live and walk in the Spirit. He is a powerful presence within us constantly helping us to see the truth.

Are you listening to the Holy Spirit directing you? His still, small voice is the one who is calling you to all truth. He wants to help you see all that is hidden and set aside just for you. Look for Him and ask Him to show you these special manifestations of His love made just for you. He will show you as you listen and obey.

The power of the Holy Spirit is active within you when you surrender your will to His. Tell Jesus that you are ready to be led by the Spirit of truth because you want all that He wants for you!

HE SPEAKS TO ME

# July 9

*"I told you that I am he.*
*So, if you seek me, let these men go."*
*John 18:8*

Jesus paid the price so that we could be set free. He did not want us to be imprisoned for our faith but prayed for us to know Him. He stepped up and endured the punishment for our sake. He suffered on the cross so we can have eternal life. He loved us so much that He took all our sins upon Himself. What a wonderful Savior we have in Jesus!

Have you ever thought about how much Jesus took upon Himself just for your sake? He paid the price for your sins. He was not afraid of what He would endure, but He took the cup that was given Him for the joy that would be ours through His resurrection.

Jesus wants you to know Him intimately. He wants to have deep conversations with you. Jesus is present in your life when you seek Him. He wants a relationship with you more than anything else. He has paid it all so that you can know true joy. Do you have your joy in Jesus? He is where the joy is!

# July 10

*"Even as the Son of Man came not to be served but to serve, and to give his life as a ransom for many."*
*Matthew 20:28*

Jesus came to serve and not to be served. He gave His life as a ransom for many to come to life. He wants us to seek to serve Him as He guides us. He rewards those who seek Him in all that they do instead of seeking to be served themselves. His hand will guide the servants to their duties in His kingdom.

Leaders serve and do not seek to be served. Will you be a leader for your Lord and Savior? All who call upon Him will be saved. All who give their hearts to Jesus will find eternal life. The lost need you to direct their hearts to hope that is eternal. Hope has a name, and His name is Jesus Christ, the Redeemer!

Where is Jesus calling you to serve? You can be a light to those who need Jesus in their lives. They are looking for hope and need to be directed to Jesus. Most do not even realize who they are missing. But you know, because you know the truth that has set you free and His name is Jesus Christ the King!

# July 11

*"For the poor you always have with you,*
*but you do not always have me."*
*John 12:8*

Jesus walks with us, and talks with us, and calls us friend. He wants to spend more time with us just as He did with His disciples. He sees our worries and wants to take them away from us. He will never give us more than we can handle when we stay closely connected to Him and His will.

Are you spending more time with Jesus each day so you can know Him and His will for you? He speaks the truth to your soul and wants you to see Him with fresh faith. He will open the door to deeper faith when you decide to trust Him fully in all that you do.

In what areas of your life do you need to trust Jesus more? He will take all those burdens you have been carrying for years now when you decide to let go and let Him step in every situation you are facing. He will keep you on the straight and narrow road with Him. It is not too late to make a detour in the direction you are going so that you can get back on the road to love and grace. It is the perfect time to give Jesus the wheel so He can help you find your way home!

# July 12

"You are those who justify yourselves before men, but God knows your hearts. For what is exalted among men is an abomination in the sight of God."
Luke 16:15

God knows all our hearts and sees our intentions and motivations. He sees when we do things for our own self-interests that are against His will. It hurts Him to see us living selfishly so that we may be exalted. The Father will discipline us when we fall out of His way of living. He wants to bring us back to Him because He loves us so much.

Those who exalt themselves will be humbled, but those who are humble will be exalted. The humble can see Jesus because they are looking for His guidance and strength to direct them in all areas of their lives. The humble choose to serve like Jesus and not be served themselves.

Are you living to exalt Jesus or yourself? Pray you would humble yourself before the Father and seek Him with all your heart. He wants to be the one to exalt you so He can do more in you than you could imagine. Bow to your knees, give Him your heart, and you will be in awe of His wonder and overcome with His glory!

# July 13

*"You see all these, do you not? Truly, I say to you,
there will not be left here one stone upon another
that will not be thrown down."*
*Matthew 24:2*

Jesus tells us to look around and be ready to see what He desires to show us. When we see with His eyes, there will be signs of the end times. He will bring light to the darkness and hope to the hopeless. It is time to return to Jesus. He will come again with glory on that day that is known only by the Father.

Will you look to see what Jesus wants you to see? He has been showing you miracles and signs every day that you have overlooked. He has given you warnings about what is to come so that you will help others believe. He has lifted you up with His compassion and mercy by giving you more than you deserve.

The love of Jesus reaches far and wide for you and will cover a multitude of sins. There is no sin too great that cannot be confessed and forgiven. It is never too late to repent and turn around. Jesus can redeem what was lost, and that includes you. Turn toward His face and He will shine His wonderful love and grace upon you!

# July 14

*"Come away by yourselves to a desolate place and rest a while."*
**Mark 6:31**

Jesus knows we need rest for our weary bodies and souls. He tells us to come to a place with Him where He can provide us the rest we so desperately need. Steal away to the place where Jesus is calling and find calmness and peace. Jesus brings restoration when we go where He leads. He assures us that all our worries will fade when we take time to pray to Him and turn our worries into prayers.

What are you worried about that has left you worn out and overburdened? Be still, right now, with Jesus. The distractions are taking over your life and causing your body to be weary. Come away with Jesus to a desolate place and find much needed rest.

Pray for the peace of Christ to enter your heart and soul. Take time out of your busy schedule to have more quiet time with Him. Jesus wants your attention, but you are too busy for Him. Those things that seem so important have taken up too much of your time. Start today by setting aside time for Jesus. He wants to spend quality time with you!

HE SPEAKS TO ME

# July 15

*"Would that you, even you had known on this day the things that make for peace! But now they are hidden from your eyes."*
*Luke 19:42*

We can all have the peace of Christ. Perfect peace is for all of us who want a relationship with Jesus. There is promised peace when we choose to receive. We do have a choice about what we will see and how we will respond to the calling of Jesus. He calls all of us into a right relationship with Him. He forgives us so that we can be free!

Have you been looking to the world for your peace? Remember that lasting peace only comes through Jesus Christ. He can give you what the world cannot give. Take heart and do not let your heart be troubled. Jesus has overcome the world to give you His everlasting peace.

What is holding you back from complete surrender to the peace of Jesus? Think about why you feel stressed today and choose to let it all go. When you do, you will start receiving peace that is freely given to you. Peace starts and ends with Jesus. Make the decision to follow Jesus and peace will follow you!

# July 16

*"Bring some of the fish that you have just caught."*
*John 21:10*

J esus knows the successes and failures that we have experienced in this life. He also knows our intentions and our desires. He will work all things out for good for those who love the Lord and are called according to His purpose. He will bring us more when we honor Him with what we have.

There is more for you in His kingdom. He wants you to fish for men so that His influence will spread and more will know the peace of Christ. You will help bring others to Jesus when you spend time in the presence of your Savior with your eyes on Him. Be caught up in the love of the Lord instead of in the challenges before you.

What have you been hoping for? Bring Jesus your requests and He will supply all that you need in His time. He knows what is before you right now and what you will be facing in the future. He will help you rise above so that you can move forward with greater faith.

# July 17

*"I in them and you in me, that they may become perfectly one, so that the world may know that you sent me and loved them even as you loved me."*
**John 17:23**

Jesus wants to be one with us as He is one with the Father. He and the Father are perfectly one. As we believe, we become one with Jesus and He will dwell in us through the power of the Holy Spirit. The Father loves us so much that He sent Jesus to love us and live with us.

Do you know how much Jesus loves you? He wants you to know the love He has for you that is evidenced by His sacrifice for all. The Father placed Him in a position to reach the world by His saving grace. He gave *all* so that you could be set free. What a wonderful Savior He is!

It is for freedom that Christ set you free, so open your heart and let His love touch you in marvelous ways. There is more for you in the arms of your Savior. Seek Him while He is near so He will draw near to you. Call upon the name of the Lord and He will speak to you.

# July 18

*"Now when these things begin to take place,*
*straighten up and raise your heads, because your*
*redemption is drawing near."*
*Luke 21:28*

Jesus gives us direction and warning about what will take place in the near future. He encourages us to look up and be ready for the time of redemption that is to come. He wants us all to be ready when the hour comes for His return so we can be redeemed. Take notice and raise your heads to see the glory that is to come!

Let perseverance finish its work in you so that Jesus can accomplish what He has purposed in you. Fulfill the ministry you have been given in the Lord and thank Him for these opportunities to bring His peace wherever He takes you.

Where will you serve until the day comes for Jesus to return? He has called you to a purpose for many more to be added to His kingdom. Do not delay or wait to do what He has put in your heart to do for Him. He will raise you and wake you up to new responsibilities. Rise up, take courage, and do it!

# July 19

*"The time is fulfilled, and the kingdom of God is at hand; repent and believe in the gospel."*
*Mark 1:15*

Jesus wants us to repent and believe in the gospel now because the kingdom of God is at hand. He knows the sins we have committed and the temptations that have tried to overcome us. But He also knows that the victory has already been won through redemptive grace that He has given us. Do not lose heart, but believe, because Jesus has overcome death and has risen victoriously for us!

Saving grace is available for you to receive when you confess your sins to Jesus and ask for His forgiveness. Fear not, for He has come to give you salvation through His sacrifice. He paid it all so you could have life everlasting!

Will you decide to follow Jesus at all costs? If so, take up your cross and follow the Savior of the world. He knows you worry so much that you cannot take your eyes off the mounting problems before you. But He calls you to take up His cross and follow Him to the light where peace and love reign forever.

# July 20

*"You will seek me and you will not find me.*
*Where I am you cannot come."*
**John 7:34**

Jesus is sitting at the right hand of the Father in heaven. He sees us as His children when we believe. He wishes for us to know Him as our Messiah. He yearns for us to seek Him. He only saves those who believe and make the choice to ask Him into their hearts. Those who do not make the choice will not be saved because they do not believe He is who He says He is.

Will you ask Jesus in your heart? If so, you will have guaranteed eternal life and His Spirit living in you. If not, you will not have salvation and will not join Him in Heaven. He wants heaven to be full of believers, and His desire and prayer is that all would be saved. He wants us all to be one with the Father as He is one with Him.

Jesus wants you to seek His heavenly treasures above instead of worldly things around you. He yearns for you to know the depth of His love. He needs you to stop focusing on other things and start trusting Him in all you do. Oh, how He loves to see your heart connected to His!

# July 21

*"Blessed are those who hunger and thirst for righteousness, for they shall be satisfied."*
*Matthew 5:6*

Those who hunger and thirst for righteousness will be blessed because they are satisfied. Blessings follow the ones who follow Jesus. He gives joy in abundance to His believers in grace. He imparts wisdom to the faithful followers who do not give up but keep their eyes on Him.

Is the comparison game of our world promoted through social media making your life miserable because you do not have what your neighbors and friends have? Do you feel worthless and depressed because of these feelings of envy? Jesus wants to lift you up and tell you not to listen to the lies spinning around in your head. Instead of looking at what you do not have, He wants you to look at Him! He sees you and wants to speak His love over you.

Yes, life is not fair and can be hard at times, but when you turn to Jesus, He will give you all you need. He is always your anchor of hope. Even in the storms of life, He will be your lifesaver. You will never hunger or thirst when you feed on His bread of life and drink His living water. He will sustain you!

# July 22

*"To you it has been given to know the secrets of the kingdom of heaven, but to them it has not been given."*
*Matthew 13:11*

J esus has given His believers the keys to the kingdom when we love Him with all our hearts. He is certain we will look to Him for all we need when our hearts are close to His. The secrets are not hidden to those who know and love Him, but are revealed in His time. When we show our love for Jesus by obeying His commandments, He manifests Himself to us in real ways.

Jesus brings peace to those who seek Him. He does not want you to fall away from Him because of people without peace around you but wants you to draw closer to Him by helping Him do work where you live. Where do you see Jesus moving in your community? Join Jesus in the work He is doing, and you will see His manifestations of love for you.

Do you feel peace from Christ or pressure from the world right now? Close your eyes, picture Jesus holding you, and breathe until you feel the stress leave your body and the arms of Jesus holding you tight.

# July 23

*"I have compassion on the crowd, because they have been with me now three days and have nothing to eat."*
**Mark 8:2**

Jesus exhibited compassion wherever He went. He saw people in need all around Him and gave them love. He was a wonderful teacher, healer, and friend. He never let anyone feel rejected or unloved. He noticed everyone and made them feel special in so many marvelous and miraculous ways!

Where do you need Jesus to help you? If you need a friend, He will talk to you and give you hope. If you need healing, He will heal you in His will and in His timing. If you need to know the truth, He will teach you all things. If you need rest, He will comfort you and bathe you in peace. Tell Him what you need, and He will shower you with compassion and mercy.

If you need Jesus, He is there for you. Just ask and you shall receive so that your joy may be full! There is no one else that will be there at every moment of your life. Stop relying on other people and other things to bring you what only Jesus can. Jesus is the one who will rescue you from falling, restore you to your salvation, and revive you with His Spirit!

# July 24

*"Yet because this widow keeps bothering me, I will give her justice, so that she will not beat me down by her continual coming."*
*Luke 18:5*

Jesus hears our persistent prayers. He knows how much we need Him in our lives, and He gives us time when we keep knocking at His door. We will find Him when we keep seeking Him. He restores every broken heart. He brings hope to every situation when we let Him in our lives. Our Lord is so great that He opens the door so we can see His light.

There are prayers left to be answered that you have yet to pray. Jesus will take notice when you keep asking with persistence. Delight in the Lord and He will give you confidence to trust in His plan and purpose for you. He always knows best, so keep leaning on Jesus for His will to be done in your life.

Jesus hears your cries and attends to the voice of your prayers. He knows you are hurting, and He wants to help you. Whenever you call, He is there. All you must do is keep seeking, asking, and knocking, and the door will open to you. What is on your heart right now? Be constant in your prayers. Jesus hears you!

# July 25

*"Lazarus, come out."*
*John 11:43*

Jesus raised His friend Lazarus from the dead. He came just in time to raise Him up from the grave and give Him life. Even when others thought He was dead, Jesus brought the miracle of life to His friend. He will give us new life when we believe and ask Him into our hearts. He will never fail us!

Where do you need encouragement right now? Is there any heaviness weighing down on you? If so, let Jesus raise you up! He is waiting for you to ask for His help so He can take the burden from you. Cast your cares onto the Lord and He will take all of them because if the Son sets you free, you are free, indeed.

Jesus will never leave or forsake you, even on your most difficult days. He loves to meet you right where you are and wants to bring joy to your heart. Count it all joy when you meet trials of various kinds, for the testing of your faith will produce steadfastness for you to stand strong and free in Jesus Christ. Your perseverance will make you complete, and you will lack nothing. You will be thanking Jesus for everything!

# July 26

*"Simon, son of John,*
*do you love me more than these?"*
**John 21:15**

Jesus is love. He loves as the Father has loved Him. He wants us to love Him as He loves us. Love is patient, love is kind. It does not envy, it does not boast, it is not proud. Love does not delight in evil but rejoices with the truth. Love never fails, but always protects, trusts, hopes, and perseveres. This kind of love is present in those who love the Lord with all their heart.

Jesus asks if you love Him more than these? If so, seek Him with all your heart because He loves you. Tell Him how much you love Him and never doubt His steadfast love for you. His love moves mountains that seem immovable. He is your way maker.

Again, Jesus is asking you if love Him more than all those other things in your life. There is more love for you than you can ever ask for or imagine with Jesus. He just wants more of your heart so that He can transform you from the inside out and show you how much love He has for you. Will you give Him your whole heart?

# July 27

*"See, you are well! Sin no more, that nothing worse*
*may happen to you."*
**John 5:14**

Jesus came to save us from our sins. He made us well again. But He knew we would be tempted to sin because the world is full of temptations and evil intentions. He asks us to repent of our sin and sin no more so that nothing worse may happen to us. He pleads for us to turn away from sin and turn to Him so we can live well.

Have your sins caused separation? Jesus wants our *'yes'* to be *'yes'* and our *'no'* to be *'no'*. Jesus gives us truth in His words in red in the Bible for us to live out daily. When we follow His commandments, we are following Christ who loves us unconditionally.

Will you choose to obey Jesus and step away from sin? In this world you will have trouble but take heart because Jesus has overcome the world. His blood ran red so that you could run free. He was wounded for your transgressions and bruised for your iniquities, but by His stripes you are healed! Sin no more and receive your healing from Jesus, the Great Physician and Healer!

# July 28

*"No servant can serve two masters, for either he will
hate the one and love the other, or he will be devoted
to the one and despise the other. You cannot serve
God and money."*
*Luke 16:13*

Jesus knows we cannot serve Him if money is our
master. We must not put any other gods before
Him. To be a servant, Jesus must be the one we
are fully devoted to in our thoughts and our actions.
He is the King of our Heart when we have heart
knowledge and not just head knowledge.

Do you just know about Jesus, or do you know Him
as your Lord and Savior? There is a difference
between just knowing about Jesus and knowing Him
as Lord. Jesus knows how much you need Him and
wants you to realize He can fill the empty places of
your heart when you choose to have a relationship
with Him.

The Holy Spirit comes into your life when Jesus fills
you up. He will remove the emptiness and replace it
with His joy. He will guide you, direct you, and teach
you with His truth. He will comfort you when you
reach out through your prayers and surrender your
heart to Him. He will never let you go!

# July 29

*"Take heart; it is I. Do not be afraid."*
*Mark 6:50*

Fear will stop us from doing what Jesus wants us to do. Fear is a liar and when we believe these lies, fear will prevent us from stretching our faith. But Jesus tells us to take heart and not be afraid because He is the one who reaches for us with outstretched arms and grabs our hand to pull us out of the storm.

For God has not given you a spirit of fear, but of power, and of love, and of self-control. Fear will leave when you let God fight your battles and stop trying to fight alone. He sees your difficulties and will turn them into opportunities to grow closer to Him if you will listen with your heart. He instructs you as you take time to pray and listen to His voice.

Is fear controlling your life? If so, it is time to let it all go. Take heart, for Jesus has come to rescue you to Himself. He sees you and knows how to help you. His love conquers all for you. Let your faith rise and all fear will disappear!

# July 30

*"Did I not tell you that if you believed you would see
the glory of God?"*
**John 11:40**

Jesus wants us to believe so we can see the glory
of God! If we lift our eyes to the hills, we will
see that our help comes from the Lord. He makes
all things new for our eyes to see and believe. The
glory of God shines upon all who make Jesus their
Lord. He opens the eyes of the blind and makes all
things brighter for all.

The light of Christ shines on all who call Jesus their
Lord. His light shines brightest in the dark. Do you
see the millions of stars created by God shining down
to light up the night sky? He made those stars for you
to know how bright His love shines upon the world.
He made those stars for you! Show Him how much
you love Him by your praises and voice of your
prayers. He made you to worship Him!

Sing praises to the Lord with the sound of your voice.
Whisper your love to Him as you lie down to sleep.
Worship the Lord as a true worshipper in spirit and in
truth. Tell the Lord how much you love Him and take
time to thank Him for all He has done for you!

# July 31

"*But the Helper, the Holy Spirit, whom the Father will send in my name, he will teach you all things and bring to your remembrance all that I have said to you.*"
*John 14:26*

Jesus gives us the Holy Spirit who teaches us all things and brings to our minds all that He says to us. The Father sent Him as a gift to all who believe in Jesus. He makes all things new for all who live with the power of the Holy Spirit in them. We are spiritually blessed and highly favored as children of the Most High.

Have you activated the Holy Spirit who lives in you? He touches you with His power when you surrender to His will. He wants the best for you and will guide you to all truth. Listen to His still, small voice guiding you. Hear Him sharing truth in love.

The Holy Spirit is your Helper. He will share His breath of love with you as you come to Him with arms wide open. He brings new hope to your situation and clears up any confusion. With Him as your guiding light, there is no darkness. Peace flows from the presence of the Holy Spirit. Receive the Holy Spirit!

Go therefore and
make disciples of all
nations,

*baptizing them*

*in the name of the*

THE FATHER,
AND THE SON,
AND THE HOLY SPIRIT.

MATTHEW 28:19

# *August 1*

*"Leave her alone, so that she may keep it for the day*
*of my burial."*
*John 12:7*

Jesus instructs us to listen and wait for Him because He does what He says He will do. He recognizes when His followers act in ways that honor Him versus acting in ways to please people. He blessed the actions of one woman who worshipped Jesus by pouring expensive ointment on His feet. Several people were wanting to save the rest of the ointment, but Jesus knew He was to die soon, and she would be able to use the rest for His burial.

It is easy to listen to the crowd when you are confused and need direction. The road of the world is wide, and the path is crowded with distractions and detours. However, when you listen through the power of the Holy Spirit to what Jesus wants you to do and stay on the straight and narrow road with Jesus, you will be blessed, indeed. Which road will you take?

The road is narrow that leads to life, but it is the only way that takes you to see the risen Jesus. Will you go where He calls you and listen to His beautiful voice calling you to action? Wait upon Jesus and listen to His promptings.

# August 2

*"You have heard that it was said,*
*'An eye of an eye and a tooth for a tooth."*
*Matthew 5:38*

We choose how we will act when others confront us. We can fight back in anger, or we can remain silent and seek Jesus. He knows how we should act and hopes we will do what He wants for us. Remember, Jesus will fight our battles time after time. He will help us when we need to know what to do. Call upon Jesus!

What are you facing that is causing you unnecessary stress? Pray for Jesus to come and take this from you so that you can rise above the fray. It is okay to be frustrated, but do not let this steal your joy. Jesus wants you to have confidence that He can take away what is bothering you and make it better. You do not have to worry or fret when Jesus is on your side.

Have you given your worries to Jesus? He wants to take them from you. He will fight your battles. Just remain silent. Try letting Jesus fight for you so you can focus on the positive things in your life! You are too blessed to be stressed!

# *August 3*

*"Abide in me, and I in you. As the branch cannot
bear fruit by itself, unless it abides in the vine,
neither can you, unless you abide in me."*
*John 15:4*

Jesus wants us to abide in Him. He knows our
faith will grow when we do. We cannot bear fruit
unless we abide in Jesus, our vine. He is the vine,
and we are the branches. He will give us spiritual
blessings and strength when we abide. We can do all
things through Him, who strengthens us with life-
giving power.

Abiding in Jesus means you seek Him in all you do.
You stay connected with Him by communicating with
Him through prayer. You read His Word of Truth and
make effort to follow the commandments in it. You
tell people how Jesus has made a difference in your
life, and you show them how they can have a deeper
relationship with Him. Are you abiding in Jesus?

Jesus knows your heart and He loves to see how
much you love Him. He knows when you abide in
Him. He asks you to keep abiding in Him so you can
bear spiritual fruit. Apart from Him, you can do
nothing. With Him, you can do anything! Decide to
abide!

# August 4

*"What God has made clean, do not call common."*
**Acts 11:9**

God has given us all the chance to be forgiven, but only if we choose Him. He wants us to be washed clean by the blood of Jesus. We can receive His forgiveness when we confess and ask for the wonder-working power of the blood to spill over us. He washes us white and makes us whole again. What God has made clean is not common, but incredible!

Do you have something weighing on you that you want to confess to the Father who forgives? Tell Him what is on your heart, and He will forgive you. He does not hold a grudge against you. In fact, He hopes you will make the choice to repent so you can be made new. Ask and you shall receive full forgiveness.

Pray to your Father who made you in His image. Let Him see how much you love Him through complete surrender. Praise Him for all His grace. He loves everything about you. He calls you worthy and wanted. Remember the promise that He will never let you go!

# August 5

*"Let these words sink into your ears: the Son of Man is about to be delivered into the hands of men."*
**Luke 9:44**

Jesus, the Son of Man, knew He would be arrested and suffer death on the cross. But He also knew that He would rise from death to life so that we could be forgiven and free. Jesus came so that we could have a saving relationship with Him and gain eternal life. What a joy it is to be saved!

Jesus promises new life to all who choose to make Him Lord. He does not discriminate but encourages all to come to Him. He wants us all to be one in Him. His promises are for you. His love is for you. Does His love quicken your heart to know Him more intimately?

Spend more time with Jesus in your Bible. He is the Word, and the Word is with Him. When you read His Word, you will know Him and love Him more deeply. He wants to talk to you. He yearns to spend time with you. Make every effort to know Him and you will receive His blessings!

# August 6

*"O woman, great is your faith!*
*Be it done for you as you desire."*
*Matthew 15:28*

Jesus sees our faith. Great faith brings us closer to Him and His will for us. He wants our faith to grow and will give us opportunities to let faith rise. Fear and doubt disappear when faith grows stronger. We see Jesus when we live by faith and not by sight because He directs us to all things, even the unknown. We do not need to know all the details when Jesus is in charge.

Are you including Him in every step of your journey? He wants to be with you in the valleys where it is difficult and, on the mountaintops, where it is joyous. By your faith, He will heal you. He will move in your heart when you embrace faith and let go of fear.

Jesus knows your heart and sees your faith. He rewards those who remain faithful. He looks far and wide to find those who have a heart after His and who will do what He needs them to do. Keep Him close and you will see things that you never thought could be possible. Nothing is too hard for Jesus!

# *August 7*

*"And I tell you, you are Peter, and on this rock I will build my church, and the gates of hell shall not prevail against it."*
*Matthew 16:18*

Jesus told Peter that He would build His church on the rock and knew that Peter would someday help Him. But He also knew Peter would deny knowing Him three times out of fear when Jesus was arrested to be put to death. Peter made mistakes and Jesus forgave Him. He gave Peter another chance to show Jesus how much he loved Him by asking Him three times if Peter loved Him. He also forgives us when we do not make the right choices.

Have you faced recent challenges in your faith and kept quiet so as not to cause conflict? When you do not speak up, you are not building up the church. Encouraging others by example to love above self is only possible when Jesus is part of your story.

People need to hear and see you proclaiming your faith by sharing Jesus wherever you are. Instead of worrying about who you might offend, make every effort to share the good news of the gospel. Do you love Jesus? Feed His sheep with love that flows from Him.

# August 8

*"Do you believe in the Son of Man?"*
**John 9:35**

The Son of Man came to earth so that He could know what it was like to live as man with the holiness of God. He had authority given to Him by the Father to live among us and bring hope to every situation. But He also had to suffer for our sins so that we could be saved. But the good news is that He conquered death and is alive so that we can live. He gives us new life when we choose to believe in Him. He does all things to bring God glory!

If Jesus were standing before you, would He find you faithful because you believe? He wants you to be a part of His kingdom and hopes that you will make the choice to stand firm with Him always. Jesus is the same today, yesterday, and always. His love remains and never changes.

Pray your boldest prayer asking the Father in the name of Jesus. He will answer you as you pray by faith. Then believe you have already received His will for you. Walk in victory because you have Jesus, the Son of Man, on your side and living in your heart.

# August 9

*"Behold, your house is forsaken. And I tell you, you will not see me until you say, 'Blessed is he who comes in the name of the Lord!'"*
*Luke 13:35*

Oh, how Jesus needs us to see Him and make Him first in our lives! We will not see Him unless we bless Him by praising Him in our homes and outside our homes. Our blessings come when we give thanks to Him for the seen and the unseen. Our faith will bring us closer to our Lord. Our homes will be a place where we can meet Jesus and feel His peace.

Do you have a place in your home where you meet Jesus and pray? He wants us to have that secret place of prayer where we shut out the world and have sweet fellowship with Him. Your place will be special to Jesus wherever it is. Find that place and meet regularly with Jesus so He can speak to you.

Jesus speaks to you when you pray and listen. He speaks when you read His Word and ask Him to show you how to apply it to your life. He will say great and mighty things to you the closer you draw to Him. Take time, pray, and listen closely for the voice of Truth.

HE SPEAKS TO ME

# August 10

*"Is a lamp brought in to be put under a basket, or under a bed, and not on a stand?"*
*Mark 4:21*

Jesus is the light of the world! We need to proclaim His love by shining His light for all to see. If we are in a dark place, we need the light to shine brightly so we can see. We would not put a light under a bed or a basket so as not to shine but would put it in a place where the light would shine the brightest! In the same way, Jesus wants to brighten up our world. Bring His light to the world, so He can light up the darkest places.

Your light will shine when you seek Jesus. He shines in and through those who seek Him and His truth in all that they do. What the world needs is more love through these dark times. Be a lantern of love to those around you.

Where can you go light your world? Your love will spark a new light that will shine in the darkness. As you spread the light, others will begin seeing the brilliant light and hearts will draw close to Jesus! Begin anew today and shine the light of Jesus. It is time to shine so all can see!

# *August 11*

*"Father, I thank you that you have heard me."*
*John 11:41*

The Father hears our prayers and petitions. He knows our needs and will always provide. He wants us to ask so He can answer us in ways that are even better than we can ever imagine. Sometimes the answer is not now because He wants us to grow our faith in the waiting room. Other times the answer is no because He has something better for us. But at times, the answer is yes, and our requests are His will for us.

Prayers cannot be answered unless you pray. All the unanswered prayers are those that have not been prayed. Think about all the prayers that you did not pray over the years. Then reflect on the ones you did pray where you got answers. Do you believe the Father heard your prayers? He bent down to hear each one and gave an answer. Every prayer is important to the Father. So, take time and lift up all of your requests.

When you do not know what to pray, the Spirit intercedes for you. The Father honors your humility and sees your devoted heart. Take time to pray and you will know the way!

# August 12

*"Go therefore and make disciples of all nations, baptizing them in the name of the Father and the Son and of the Holy Spirit."*
*Matthew 28:19*

The Great Commission is an instruction for us to go into the world and make disciples. When we make disciples, we fulfill part of our commission. But the second part of that command is to baptize them in the name of the Father, the Son, and the Holy Spirit. Once a believer makes the decision to follow Jesus, we can help that person seal their faith by the ordinance of baptism to outwardly show a committed heart to Christ.

Think about your baptism and how you felt when Jesus came into your heart. Jesus knew your surrender would give you an open and willing heart, and that when He touched you and poured joy into your soul you could walk and live by the power of the Spirit every moment.

Thank Jesus for making you whole again. Praise Him for filling the empty places of your heart, and then ask Him where you need to go to help fulfill His kingdom calling.

# *August 13*

*"Gather up the leftover fragments,
that nothing may be lost."*
*John 6:12*

There is nothing wasted when we do the work of Jesus. His kingdom is glorious, and He wants all to come to Him. The time is now to seek and save the lost. Even the leftover fragments can make a huge difference in the lives of those who may be looking for hope. We can be the people who give from our hearts even from what is leftover.

Jesus is always with you, even in the hardest of times. He wants you to carry on with newfound joy and finish the work He has given you. Work heartily with all your strength, working for the praise of the Lord and not people. Do not grow weary of doing good, for at the proper time, you will reap what you sow. Jesus never leaves His children, and He will never leave you!

Remember, Jesus will equip you with all you need to make disciples. He is counting on you to use your God-given gifts, so find a need and fill it while there is still time to make a difference for His kingdom glory!

# *August 14*

*"Simon son of John, do you love me?"*
*John 21:16*

Jesus loves us so much that He gives us second
chances to show our love for Him. He knew that
Simon Peter, His disciple, loved Him even after
denying knowing Jesus three different times. He
asked Simon, son of John, if He loved Him three
times to give Him a chance to proclaim His love back
to Jesus with an outpouring of emotion and
commitment to serve.

Do you love Jesus? Show Him how much you love
Him today. Show Him how your love runs deep and
wide by drawing closer to His love that conquers all.
Let His love penetrate all the places in your heart that
need healing. He will heal you spiritually and set your
heart on fire when you show and tell Him that you
love Him.

Jesus will reset your priorities and give you new
opportunities to show your love. He knows how busy
you are, but He also knows how much love you have
to give. Let your light shine before others so they may
see your good works and glorify your Father. Be a
difference-maker by sharing His love!

# *August 15*

*"Today this Scripture has been fulfilled in your
hearing."*
*Luke 4:21*

Jesus fulfills His Scripture, so be alert and stay
awake, because He is sharing truth in love. What
was written before is coming to pass for all to
see. Believe what you hear about the Messiah and
follow Him to freedom. The Scripture is truth for us
to write on our hearts and obey with our hands and
feet.

Have you read the Scripture with ears to hear what
Jesus is telling you? Open your Bible and read it with
new eyes focused on what the Holy Spirit wants you
to know. He will reveal things to you. He will share
ways that you can apply the scriptures to your daily
life.

The Bible is living and active. It is sharper than a
two-edged sword piercing to the division of soul and
spirit. It is truth for you to cling to always. All
Scripture is God-breathed and is useful for teaching,
rebuking, correcting, and training so that you will be
equipped for every good work for the sake of Christ.
Keep reading it and you will be blessed as you learn
how to live righteously.

# August 16

*"Blessed are those who are persecuted for righteousness' sake, for theirs is the kingdom of heaven."*
*Matthew 5:10*

Jesus was persecuted and knew what it is like to be attacked and disliked for righteousness' sake. He was abused and punished for no reason. But Jesus never faltered in His faith. He always remained faithful and loved all, even those who caused Him pain and suffering. He asked the Father to forgive all for they did not know what they were doing. He loved His enemies and prayed for them.

Jesus will give you courage to face your accusers with forgiveness in your heart. He will take away any offense and replace it with empathy. You will be able to rise up with wings like eagles and run with endurance even in the face of false accusations. Stay the course and you will find your heart full with His perfect peace beyond all human understanding.

He tells you that you will be blessed when you are persecuted for His sake. He knows why you are being attacked and will bring good out of the all the hurtful actions against you. Stay faithful to Jesus. Your hurt will leave when Jesus lifts you up.

HE SPEAKS TO ME
**235**

# August 17

*"Daughter, your faith has made you well; go in peace, and be healed of your disease."*
**Mark 5:34**

Oh, how Jesus loves us! He wants to help all of us reach Him so He can heal us. When we touch Him with our heart, mind, and soul, we find peace that floods our entire being! This peace will fill us up to the point that nothing and no one can stop us from rising up from the pain and discomfort of our situations. We can never be separated from His love! That is a promise worth placing our faith upon!

Do you believe that you can be healed? If you are struggling to believe, remember the daughter who ran to reach Jesus just to touch the fringe of His garment. She knew He had the power to heal, and she did not let fear stop her from touching Him. She had faith even when others questioned her healing and doubted that she would ever be made clean. Jesus healed her because of her faith.

Through your actions, have you shown Jesus that you have faith even when it seems impossible? Act like you believe the healing has happened even before it takes place. Pray in faith knowing that Jesus heals. Give your heart to the One who never leaves you.

# August 18

*"If then you have not been faithful*
*in the unrighteous wealth,*
*who will entrust to you the true riches?"*
*Luke 16:11*

Jesus wants us to bring friends to our Savior when He places them in our lives. We can invite them to know Jesus by sharing His love in our actions and by sharing our testimony of how Jesus has changed our hearts. He wants all to know Him as Lord. He will see our faith and reward our efforts when it is for true riches and not personal gain. Jesus knows our thoughts and our hearts. He helps those who remain righteous and seek true heavenly riches.

Will you help those who Jesus puts in your life? He knows how much you love Him and wants others to know His eternal love. Be devoted to Jesus in all that you do, and He will share truth in love with you. There are still things He wants to show you when you make time for Him. He is speaking to you. Is your heart turned toward Him so that you can hear His voice?

Jesus gives to those who earnestly seek Him. Bless the Lord with what He has given you and He will fill your cup to the fullest!

# *August 19*

*"Son, your sins are forgiven."*
*Mark 2:5*

We all long to hear these words, "Your sins are forgiven." We want to know that our sins are washed away and that we are clean from the inside out. Jesus came so we can be forgiven and free. Our freedom was not given so we could keep indulging in the flesh, but so we can walk in the Spirit using our freedom to serve one another humbly in love. Once we are forgiven, we are made new in Christ and no longer walk in the sins of our flesh, but in the power of the Holy Spirit who dwells within us!

Do you know that as a believer your sins are forgiven? You are no longer a slave to sin but are alive by the grace of God. He gave you Jesus so you could escape the weight of sin and live with faith and freedom and no longer be bound up with chains that you once carried with you. The old self is gone when you put on your new self after the likeness of Jesus Christ.

When you live with Jesus Christ in you, He will make you a different person who lives to serve and not to be served. And as His faithful follower, He will show you how much He loves and forgives you.

# *August 20*

*"If a kingdom is divided against itself,
that kingdom cannot stand."*
*Mark 3:24*

Jesus knew we were sinners, so He came to bring us life and healing. He calls us all to Himself so we can be united and not divided against one another. When He sees people fighting and serving only themselves, He knows betrayal, hate, and heartache will be present as well. God made us to be one with Him and to follow Him together. He commanded us to love one another as He has loved us. He also commanded us to pray for our enemies in this troubled world.

Where can you be a peacemaker where God has placed you? There are many who need to hear that Jesus is alive! The tomb is empty because Jesus has risen from death to life. He conquered death to give us life!

Have you wanted to share the gospel but are too afraid to speak up because of what people might think of you? Remember Jesus gives you the words to say and the opportunities to share. You might just be that one person who makes a difference in another person's life.

# *August 21*

*"He said to him, 'If they do not hear Moses and the Prophets, neither will they be convinced if someone should rise from the dead.'"*
*Luke 16:31*

Jesus knew there would be people who did not have ears to hear Him just like there are some who did not hear Moses and the Prophets before Him. Even so, He knows us and wants us to know Him as our Lord and Savior! There will be people in our lives who doubt and have little faith in the risen Jesus. There will be scoffers and unbelievers who deny the Savior. But we are more than conquerors who can rise above and proclaim the good news even among the negativity around us.

Where can you proclaim freedom from Christ to the captives? Think about people you know who do not have a relationship with Jesus. Jesus is calling you to go and tell your story of life renewed and restored through the saving faith of Jesus. Share the truth that Jesus can set the captives free by His redeeming grace and bring hope to the hopeless with His prevailing promises.

Will you share the hope that is in you? Jesus is listening to your heart and sees your faith.

# *August 22*

*"Therefore, stay awake, for you do not know on what day your Lord is coming."*
*Matthew 24:42*

When we are close to Jesus, we experience peace with Him. He gives us peace in the depth of our soul as we seek Him with all that is within us. He also promises He will return at an hour we least expect, so we need to stay awake and be ready for His coming. What a glorious celebration it will be when we meet Jesus face to face!

Listen with your heart to Jesus calling you to come to Him. He is going to return to take His believers home on the Day of the Lord. He wants you to be with Him so He can bring you to heaven where there is no more weeping, pain, or heartache. There is no way to describe what you will see and experience, but you can be sure that you will want to be with Jesus and not left behind. Will you awaken to His voice and be sure that you are saved?

Another blessing to look forward to is that you will meet those who have fallen asleep before you in the air upon His coming. Jesus will bring all the believers to the place He has prepared for us so we will be together forever with Him. Hallelujah!

HE SPEAKS TO ME
**241**

# *August 23*

*"And will not God give justice to his elect, who cry to him day and night? Will he delay long over them?*
*Luke 18:7*

God wants all our heart so He can give us wisdom and justice. He hears our cries and will answer in His time and in His will. We are holding on to stress because we have not let go of our worries but are still letting them control us. That stress is creating distance from God because our focus is on the problem and not the solution. God provides a way out when we seek His will and His plan of escape from the bad influences weighing us down.

What is heavy on your heart? Give this issue to Jesus who will provide you a clearer picture and how to handle it. He has been through more than any problem you will face, and He knows how tough life can be. He can give the solution you have been looking for when you ask. He will open the door and let the light in!

Is there someone or something taking you away from Jesus? Are you relying on the world to give you the answers instead of depending on Jesus? The problems of this world are real, but the answer to every question will always be clearer with Jesus!

# *August 24*

*"You are witnesses of these things."*
**Luke 24:48**

We will be witnesses of the things that Jesus wants to show us when we share our heart with Him. He speaks over things with authority and love because He is love. We will witness miracles of love if we believe in Him. We will witness lives changed by love if we trust and obey Him. We will witness salvation from love if we repent and accept His love. We are saved by His grace out of His love.

Do you know the saving grace of Jesus? He is always extending grace no matter what the sin. He gives grace upon grace so that you can walk in freedom. It is for freedom that Christ came. He wants to save you from the pain and shame of sin so you can walk freely in His love. Fall deeper into His arms of grace and let Him lavish you from head to toe.

Look in the mirror and see Jesus reflected in your face. Do you see His love cleansing all the stains of sin? His light has made you shine so people see Jesus living in you. That smile on your face is evidence of the redeeming love Jesus has given you. Jesus lives in you because He lives!

HE SPEAKS TO ME
**243**

# August 25

*"Go; your son will live."*
**John 4:50**

Jesus saved those who needed healing even if they were not in His presence. He spoke with authority to a father who wanted healing for his son who lived miles away. He could heal from a distance because He was Lord. The Son of God brought life to death and beauty from ashes. His compassion was great for people that He ministered to. He saw their needs and He met each one of them. He spoke healing over disease, and people were healed. He commanded evil to leave, and it departed. The Savior came and conquered death on the cross so that we could see evidence of life and victory in Jesus. Jesus heals!

His sons and daughters are healed today as well. Do you need healing? Ask Jesus to help you and have faith that He will do it. Even in the most difficult situation, Jesus is alive to heal you. His touch brings peace. His voice brings comfort. His eyes bring light. His love brings contentment.

Ask Jesus for what you need, and He will answer you. He does what He says He will do, and He always cares about you. He revives and restores.

# August 26

*"Whoever believes and is baptized will be saved, but whoever does not believe will be condemned."*
*Mark 16:16*

D o we believe or do we not believe? Jesus asks each of us this life-altering question. Whoever believes and is baptized will be saved, but whoever does not will be condemned. Jesus hopes we will follow Him and believe but does not force His way upon us. He will keep pursuing us until we let Him in our hearts and follow Him to freedom.

When you are facing a hard decision, will you follow Jesus' way, or will you choose your own way? The choice you make will set the course for the rest of your life. You have many ways you can go, but only one way leads to Jesus. He will hold your hand so you will not be afraid anymore. He will never let you go.

Where do you go to find your rest? If you know Jesus, you can come to Him and He will give you rest for your weary soul. If you do not, there will be restlessness in your soul and stress pulling you down. But there is a light shining upon you. Choose the Light of the World, Jesus Christ, so He can make His home in you forever!

# *August 27*

*"Whoever is not with me is against me, and whoever does not gather with me scatters."*
*Luke 11:23*

If we are not with Jesus, we are against Him because we leave Him out of our lives and we make our own plans without thinking about Jesus. He knows we need Him but will choose our own interests if we are not one with Him. Jesus wants to be present in our hearts and yearns for us to stay with Him so He can build us up. Be brave and stay with Jesus who always calls us to Himself so we will be closer to His heart.

Put Jesus first and watch how He encourages you to go the extra mile. He gives you power when weariness sets in and hope when you feel hopeless. He will strengthen you in your inner being with all spiritual blessings and enlighten your eyes so that you can see all He wants to do in you. Let Jesus gather you up and bring you straight into His loving arms.

Are you settling securely in the arms of Jesus? He wants to hold you and protect you. He will teach you how to pray so you can rise above all the stresses before you. Look closely at His wonderful face and He will shine down His perfect peace on you!

# August 28

*"Strive to enter through the narrow door. For many, I tell you, will seek to enter and will not be able."*
**Luke 13:24**

The narrow door leads right to Jesus. He is waiting on the other side for those who have asked Him in their hearts. He hears us knocking and will let us in because we have believed and are ready to receive His instructions to serve His kingdom. We come when we are called and give because we have been given so much. Jesus came for us so we could walk through the door to life and be forgiven and free.

Many will not know His joy because they have chosen the wrong door. But you know the truth and He has set you free. Keep walking in the Spirit who brings life and set aside the flesh that leads to death. The flesh and the Spirit are against each other and cannot exist in your heart at the same time. Follow Jesus. Is the spirit or the flesh stronger in you?

When you say yes to Jesus, He will give you a new heart and put a new spirit in you. The Holy Spirit will come alive in you to give power that trumps all the temptations of the flesh.

# *August 29*

*"Unless you see signs and wonders you will not believe."*
**John 4:48**

There are many who only believe when they see things happen. We are people who need to see to believe because we want human understanding. Jesus knows many who lack faith and will only believe when they see signs and wonders. He came to save us all so He will keep speaking to us until we finally hear Him and believe without seeing.

Whose voice are you listening to? You will listen to the one who is more prevalent in your heart. Jesus wants to be the voice you hear and obey. He is speaking love to you because He is love. He is always faithful and will reward those who stay faithful to Him even when fear and uncertainty come to the surface.

Do you have faith? Faith is being sure of what you hope for and certain of things not yet seen. Faith believes even without knowing all the details. Faith rises even in the face of fear. Faith deepens in the heart of those who follow the author and perfecter of faith, Jesus Christ, our King!

# August 30

*"See my hands and my feet, that it is I myself.*
*Touch me, and see. For a spirit does not have flesh*
*and bones as you see that I have."*
*Luke 24:39*

Jesus was wounded for our transgressions and bruised for our iniquities. By His stripes we are healed. He secured peace for us by His pain, suffering, and death on the cross so we could be saved. He showed the doubting disciples proof the tomb was empty because He rose from death to life. He wanted them to touch Him. He brought peace standing before His friends with scarred hands and feet. His touch opened their doubting hearts to His abounding love.

"Receive the Holy Spirit!" Jesus spoke these words as He appeared to His friends after the resurrection. As He spoke, He breathed on them. He wanted them to have the supernatural power present through the Holy Spirit. Jesus would not be walking with thcm but would empower them with His Spirit inside them.

Will you receive the Holy Spirit? Will you touch Jesus with your heart? Jesus will not deny you before the Father when you receive Him. He has overcome the world!

# August 31

*"See that you say nothing to anyone, but go, show yourself to the priest and offer the gift that Moses commanded, for a proof to them."*
*Matthew 8:4*

The saving grace and healing power of Jesus is for all. He heals those He loves with compassion and grace. He sees those who need healing and pours grace over them. If we want healing, we can ask in the name of Jesus, believing that it is done. It is our choice to thank Him for the healing before we see it and praise Him for giving us healing by His grace. He sees all of our struggles and He knows how to heal us. Will we stay and pray for His healing to come to us for the glory of God to be revealed?

When your prayers are answered, do you give thanks? Jesus hopes to see your thankful heart because it shows your gratitude for things He has done. He wants to see your praise and thanksgiving.

Remember the last-answered prayer and thank Him now for what He did for you. Believe He will do it again! Write down another prayer on your heart. Remember his faithfulness. With Jesus, all things are possible!

FOR GOD
*so loved*
THE WORLD, THAT HE
*he gave his only Son,*
that whoever believes
IN HIM
*should have eternal*
LIFE.
JOHN 3:16

# September 1

*"Take heart, my son; your sins are forgiven."*
*Matthew 9:2*

Jesus forgives and forges deeper relationships with His followers when they listen and obey Him. He desires to reach people who love Him and seek to know Him better. When He sees our faith rising, He rewards us with knowing more of Him. He speaks life over death and hope over defeat. He wants us to take heart because He loves us so much!

Where have you seen Jesus working in your life? Have you laid your sins at the cross? He wants to forgive you and remove the sins that shackle you. Trust Him and let His love and forgiveness wipe away every ounce of guilt and shame. Repent and you will hear the chains fall off. The sound of chains breaking is beautiful to His ears.

Let it all go and be free. It is for freedom that Christ has set us free. You are no longer bound by the sin that has held you back from a closer walk with Jesus. You are forgiven because Jesus took all your sins when He died and rose again on the third day. He came so you could walk and live freely forgiven by the blood He shed for you. Will you let Jesus break every chain?

# September 2

*"And no one puts new wine into old wineskins. If he does, the wine will burst the skins—and the wine is destroyed, and so are the skins. But new wine is for fresh wineskins."*
*Mark 2:22*

Jesus brings new life to those who trust Him as Lord. Jesus gives fresh faith and abiding love to those who decide to faithfully follow Him. He promises peace to those who put the kingdom of God first. He grants strength to those whose joy is in Him. Where the Spirit of the Lord is, there is freedom, and our old ways will no longer be the way we want to live.

Do you want to rededicate your life to Christ? He has been waiting for you. When you walk with newness of joy and peace from above with the guiding light of Jesus, you will be made new in Christ. You have no need for the old ways anymore.

Stay focused on the Spirit and He will bless you richly. New wine cannot be put into old wineskins, so keep moving forward in your faith, not backwards. It is by faith that you will bear much fruit. Trust Him and you will see the bountiful harvest appear in your life!

# September 3

*"Truly, I say to you, among those born of women there has arisen no one greater than John the Baptist. Yet the one who is least in the kingdom of heaven is greater than he."*
*Matthew 11:11*

Jesus talks about who is the greatest among those born of women. John the Baptist was the man who came as a messenger to prepare the way before us. John the Baptist called the people to repent because the kingdom of God was at hand. Jesus also reminded His listeners that whoever is least in the kingdom of heaven is even greater. For Christ's kingdom is not for those who exalt themselves, but for those who humble themselves before the mighty hand of God.

Have you humbled yourself before God? He is working in your heart when you bow in humility. He will clear a path for you to work effectively and efficiently. His favor is upon your efforts because you have chosen His way.

Jesus asks His own to eat with Him at His table of grace. Jesus wants to commune with you because you have made Him Lord of your life. He wants to share life with you, His beloved!

# September 4

*"Do not think I have come to bring peace to the earth. I have not come to bring peace, but a sword."*
*Matthew 10:34*

Jesus came to bring a spiritual peace among His faithful. He taught us that His presence on earth would bring division and not peace among the people on earth and there is a cost when we decide to follow Jesus. Those who decide to follow Him will experience persecution and hatred at times. But, when we do make our home with Savior, we will experience a lasting spiritual peace.

Are you looking for peace the world cannot give? Jesus knows you are hurting and wants to give you His peace now. He is telling you to receive His peace and be still. Listen to His peaceful voice and rest in His presence knowing He is holding you tight. His everlasting love will bless your broken heart and touch your weary soul.

Come to the Prince of Peace right now. Tell Him what is bothering you and hear His comforting words pulling you close. Jesus is there for you anytime you need Him. He never leaves or forsakes you. He knows what is bothering you and will make the pain go away if you ask Him.

HE SPEAKS TO ME

# September 5

*"It is said, 'You shall not put the Lord your God to the test."*
*Luke 4:12*

God does not want us to test Him. Some may try to question the Lord because they do not like what is happening to them. Others may try to understand why, so they make compromises and do not obey what God tells them to do. Frustration and selfishness enter the hearts of those who want God to prove Himself. Testing is a lack of trust.

Even if you are facing a trial, do not try to test your Lord. He will call you faithful if you trust Him through whatever you are experiencing. If He tests you in the trial, stay the course and stay faithful, and He will bring you to the other side of the challenge. He promises to always be with you.

Will God find you faithful like Jesus when He was tempted? Jesus turned away from temptation and toward God and remembered that God always provides a way out, but only if He remained faithful to God. There will be times when you need counsel, so trust God to give you the courage to face your giant. He is bigger than any giant you will ever face!

# September 6

***"No more of this!"***
***Luke 22:51***

Misplaced anger causes people to act in ways that are not pleasing to the Lord. He does not want us to do hurtful things because we are angry and offended. Instead, He hopes we forgive and move forward knowing that vengeance belongs to the Lord. He will avenge for us so we can seek His direction before we act in difficult circumstances.

Has someone offended you so much that you are considering fighting back even without seeking the Lord's guidance? Pray that you will seek Him before you act in ways that are disrespectful to what the Lord wants. Pray for the person who has come against you and be the one who turns away from the fight. You will hear His instructions if you listen patiently.

Those who wait upon the Lord will hear Him speaking instruction and will not fear 'what ifs' of life. The one who is patient will find the peace that is needed in any circumstance. Be one who hears the Lord because you trust in Him for all you need and then peace will rule in your heart.

# September 7

*"It was not that this man sinned, or his parents, but that the works of God might be displayed in him."*
**John 9:3**

When a man was born blind, many asked Jesus if the man sinned or his parents sinned because he had no sight. Jesus answered that neither he, nor his parents sinned, but that he was born that way so the glory of God could be displayed in him. Jesus was going to perform a miracle healing of this blind man for the glory of God to be revealed so people would believe that He was truly the Son of God.

Do you believe in miracles? Jesus has miracles for you, too. He wants you to believe He can and *will* perform them for God's glory to be revealed. There is nothing too hard for Jesus. Know that He can perform miracle healings for you like He did for the blind man.

Can you imagine yourself healed from whatever you are facing now? Thank Jesus for the healing He has in His hands and trust Him to give you that perfect healing in His time. Keep praying and know that He hears you and will bring you peace while you are waiting to experience His glory!

# September 8

*"What man of you, having a hundred sheep, if he has lost one of them, does not leave the ninety-nine in the open country, and go after the one that is lost, until he finds it?"*
*Luke 15:4*

Jesus does not rest until He finds the lost. He lives to save. He wants everyone to know Him as Lord and Savior and receive salvation. He will not stop seeking us until we come to Him with arms wide open for Him to embrace us. This is a beautiful picture of grace for all to see how Jesus loves us. He will never stop looking for the lost to come home to His heart.

Have you ever lost something of value and could not rest until you found it? In the same way, Jesus constantly seeks the one who is lost. You can aid the search and help spread the love of Jesus by directing lost people straight into the arms of Jesus. He will welcome them as He welcomed you.

Think of someone who needs Jesus. Ask the Lord to reveal that person to you. Now make every effort to bring that person to Jesus by praying fervently and patiently for them to find the truth. Share His joy and expect to see a miracle!

# September 9

*"Why do you call me good?*
*No one is good except God alone."*
**Mark 10:18**

Jesus wants us to see how God alone is good. Jesus knew people wanted Him to show them how good He was by following man's traditions and rules. Jesus did not need to prove His worth to these people or live by their standards. He pointed to God's goodness and glory so they would focus on God's holiness and righteousness. We must focus on God to see our need for a Savior. Then we will see that all have sinned and fallen short of the glory of God. We all *need* a Savior!

Do you need to repent and ask God to forgive you? If so, tell Him, and lay it down at the cross. He will take your burden and help you see that He is the only way. Give your body to God as a living sacrifice. He wants to be in your life.

Freedom reigns when Christ reigns in you. Stop trying to do things without Him. He calls you worthy and wants you to trust Him for all you need. He wants you to see how beautiful you are to Him. He will never stop loving you, dear child, so come quickly and lay it all down at His feet.

# September 10

**"Why do you question in your hearts?"**
**Luke 5:22**

Jesus knows some will question in their hearts. Unbelief and doubt are real, and He knows we will need more faith to grow closer to Him. Faith in action is the assurance of things hoped for, and the certainty of things not seen. Jesus will help us see so doubt does not arise in our hearts. Draw closer to Jesus through trusting Him wholeheartedly. Look with spiritual eyes and He will manifest Himself in marvelous and supernatural ways.

Do you still have unbelief? If so, Jesus wants to help you see with eyes of faith. He knows what you are facing now and what test is about to come into your life. Will He find you faithful when the testing comes? Pray for Jesus to help your unbelief and rise with new hope and confidence for what He is going to do in you.

How can you grow your faith? Ask Jesus to show you how and then pray for His empowerment to instill an unfaltering belief. He will enlighten you to see spiritually through the Holy Spirit's power within you. He does what He says He will do, so pray, and believe that He will open the eyes of your heart!

# September 11

*"For God so loved the world, that he gave his only Son, that whoever believes in him should not perish but have eternal life."*
*John 3:16*

God loved us all so much He gave us His Son, so whoever believed in Him would be saved and have eternal life. He gives each of us this special gift. God washes away our sins when we ask Jesus in our heart to be our Lord. He promises that whoever believes in Him will be saved. What a glorious promise we can cling to forever!

Jesus died and rose again so you could have a relationship with Him and live close to Him forever. He came so *you* can have eternal life if you believe. Will you receive His love and share His love? He is waiting to receive you as one of His own.

Call upon the Lord and stay close to Him. *He will answer you.* When you receive Him as Lord, He will raise you up in victory so you can live with His power present in you. You are worthy of His love. Give Him your heart and give Him the glory for saving you. Seek Him above all else and you will live forever with Him!

# September 12

*"But when the grain is ripe, at once he puts in the sickle, because the harvest has come."*
**Mark 4:29**

There is an immediate need for laborers for the harvest. The harvest is ripe, and it is time for us to work together for God's kingdom. He needs us all to do His will and work for His glory. God will give us opportunities to share His love so people will know how much they are loved. He wants us to live and work in unity so that we can do more for His kingdom purposes.

Will you seek ways you can be a kingdom builder? Listen to God calling you to His greater plan and purpose. He will show you where He can use you and will give you strength to finish His work. Many are struggling and need the love of Jesus. Look around you and see where God needs you. There are people in your community and your neighborhood who are counting on you to bring them to Jesus.

Be a difference-maker by being present. You will never regret how much you served Jesus. Keep serving faithfully, so that when you stand before Jesus, He will reward you and tell you what a good and faithful servant you have been.

HE SPEAKS TO ME

# September 13

*"I ask you, is it lawful on the Sabbath to do good or do harm, to save life or to destroy it?"*
**Luke 6:9**

Many people questioned whether Jesus could heal on the Sabbath. They wanted to accuse Him of wrongdoing. Jesus challenged their legalistic way of keeping the Sabbath holy. Jesus stated it was not unlawful to save a life or help someone by healing them, even if on the Sabbath. When people need healing, Jesus heals them.

When you are questioned for doing good, seek the Lord and His strength, and He will tell you how to respond. There are people who will question and persecute you, but your defense is the Spirit of the Lord who leads you. Keep seeking the Lord and He will give you the words He wants you to speak to your accusers.

Jesus will be with you to the end of the age. He will never leave you but will give you the courage to stand firm with Him by your side. He knows what is right and will give you the words to say to bring the truth to light. Stay positive and Jesus will encourage and build you up for what He needs you to do.

# *September 14*

*"And if you have not been faithful in that which is
another's, who will give you that which is your
own?"*
*Luke 16:12*

Jesus wants us to be faithful and take special care
when He gives us assignments. He asks us to be
faithful in the little things, so we can be entrusted
to be faithful in the big things. Little faith begets
bigger faith. We will be a trusted disciple by doing
what Jesus calls us to do. It all begins with having
faith!

Is your life evidence of great faith? Showing your
faithfulness in every situation will please God and
bring glory to Him. He needs you to remain faithful
and fruitful for His work. Your joy will be evident
when you are doing what He has called you to do.

Where is Jesus leading you to more faithful service?
Think about your life and what Jesus needs you to
accomplish for His glory. He has good works for you
to complete and a purpose and a plan for you. He
knows the plans He has for you, plans for a future and
a hope. Jesus will see you through it if He brings you
to it! Trust His plan!

# *September 15*

*"This illness does not lead to death. It is for the glory of God, so that the Son of God may be glorified through it."*
*John 11:4*

In this life, we will experience illness and pain that does not lead to death, but we may suffer so the glory of God may be seen by all when the healing comes. The Son of God will be glorified through the miracle. God works all things out for good for those who love the Lord and are called according to His purpose. Pray for God's will and consider the sufferings of this present time are not worth comparing with the glory that is to be revealed to us.

Where is your struggle right now? Know God will deliver you from the pain and defend you from your enemies. There is nothing that can stop God's ever-present protection and peace over you. Take refuge in Him.

Bring your request for healing to God and He will hear you. Tell Him what you need and wait for His answers. He will show you how much He loves you as He helps and heals you. His steadfast love is better than life, so praise Him with your lips!

# September 16

*"So therefore, any one of you who does not*
*renounce all that he has cannot be my disciple."*
**Luke 14:33**

Jesus wants us to be His disciple. He calls us to renounce all we have so we can serve Him as He wishes. There is a cost for following Jesus and making Him Lord over our life, but the joy we receive is greater and worth any sacrifice. Jesus is the way to great joy. No one can steal this joy.

Did you know that for the joy set before Him, Jesus endured the cross and disregarded its shame so you could be set free and have everlasting life? He took on all the pain and the suffering so you would know the joy that does not depend on circumstances, but on the promise of eternal life with Him. He is seated at the right hand of the Father interceding prayer for you.

Tell Jesus how much you love Him. Feel His presence touch the depths of your soul and hear His loving voice calling you to be a disciple. He wants you to abide in Him so that you can know His unending love and incredible power of the Holy Spirit. Be a disciple of Christ and you will never walk alone!

# September 17

*"No one puts a piece of unshrunk cloth on an old garment, for the patch tears away from the garment, and a worse tear is made."*
***Matthew 9:16***

When we put on Jesus and make Him Lord of our heart, He cannot be taken off of us. Jesus transforms the old self and puts on the new self after we surrender and invite Him to live in our heart. We are clothed with holiness from God, grace from Jesus Christ, and sealed with the power of love from the Holy Spirit. We are created new in Christ with all power and glory forever!

Are you living in the power that has set you free? As believers, we are given freedom to live and walk with the Spirit. But we will also be tempted to put on the old habits if we surround ourselves with people who are not close to Christ. They will try to influence us to live their way instead of Christ's way. Let go of your former way of life before you were His, and keep living in the power and presence of Christ who adores you and wants what is best for you.

What can you take off to keep close to Christ? Step out of self and step into more of Christ!

# September 18

*"You know that after two days the Passover is coming, and the Son of Man will be delivered up to be crucified."*
*Matthew 26:2*

Jesus told His disciples what He would face and when it would happen. He looked out for His friends and wanted them to understand. They still could not comprehend all that Jesus spoke to them and sometimes had doubt in their hearts. He knew they would be disheartened when He was delivered up to be crucified, but He also believed they would grow in their faith.

Jesus has given you, His faithful follower, the gift of the Holy Spirit so that you can live and work with power from above to do what seems impossible. His strength allows you to find the words to say and the actions to take even in the most difficult circumstances. He will provide endurance and the strength to accomplish what He gives you.

What impossible task is before you now? Surrender your will to His and let go of trying to figure it out all by yourself. You have a Helper, the Holy Spirit, who gives you the power and wisdom to do the right thing. Pray for guidance and He will show you the way.

HE SPEAKS TO ME

# September 19

*"Today this Scripture has been fulfilled in your hearing."*
*Luke 4:21*

Jesus states that the Scripture from the prophet Isaiah was being fulfilled by the Messiah, Jesus Christ. He was the One predicted by the prophet to fulfill it. This Scripture Jesus read to the people included prophesy about healing, rescue, judgment on sin, and the good news for all. Those who listened were confused and amazed, but their eyes were focused directly on Jesus who opened and read the scroll of the prophet.

Imagine you were there listening to Jesus. Read these words out loud with hope in your heart, "The Spirit of the Lord is upon me, because He has anointed me to proclaim good news to the poor. He has sent me to proclaim freedom for the prisoners and recovery of sight for the blind, to set the oppressed free, to proclaim the year of the Lord's favor."

Let these words sink in for you. Believe that Jesus came to bring good news for you right now no matter the circumstances you are facing. Know that He has set you free! Do not wait until everything lines up in your mind, but today, rededicate your heart to Jesus!

# September 20

*"If you were blind, you would have no guilt; but now that you say, 'We see,' your guilt remains."*
*John 9:41*

If we are spiritually blind, we cannot see what Jesus wants to do in us. He encourages us to pray for sight to see the truth. He wants us to open the eyes of our heart so He can deposit His Spirit in us. He seals His own with His Spirit and gives them spiritual power to see. His way leads to life even with detours. We can see when we look to Him and walk where He leads us.

Are you having trouble seeing because the world is trying to darken your life with lies? The enemy comes to steal, kill, and destroy and will try to blind you. Remember Jesus came to bring life so you can live in truth and light! Keep close to the light and stay on the path with Jesus.

Watch out for false prophets. You will know these people by their fruits. Watch and see what fruit they bear for the kingdom. You cannot gather grapes from thorn bushes and figs from thistles. Every tree that does not bear good fruit is cut down and thrown into the fire. Again, you will know them by their fruits so be watchful and keep your eyes open.

# September 21

*"I knew that you always hear me, but I said this on account of the people standing around, that they may believe that you sent me."*
**John 11:42**

Jesus prayed to the Father to help us when we doubted and had little faith. He knew we would need more faith in this world where people are self-centered, so He prayed persistently for us. He believed the Father would hear His requests and answer His prayers. He wanted us to know how much we are loved so He asked the Father to show us mercy and help us. He interceded to His Father on our behalf because He wanted us all to be saved.

The Father loved you so much that He gave His only Son so that when you believed you would have everlasting life. God is love and He promised to hold you as His own for eternity. What joy is found in Jesus when you are His child!

Did you know Jesus has prayed for you to know Him as your Lord and have a relationship with Him? He will never give up on you. He yearns for you to be saved so He will keep praying for you. Jesus wants you to come home to Him. He will never let you go!

# September 22

***"If you love me, you will keep my commandments."***
***John 14:15***

Jesus wants us to love Him as He has loved us. When we love Him with all that is within us, we want to keep His commandments. He will know we love Him by the way we trust in the Lord with all our heart. He will see us love Him when we acknowledge Him in all our ways. He will make our path clearer when He is first in our lives. When we choose to live obediently, it pleases Jesus.

What direction are you going? Listen to His will for you and keep heading where He leads you. He will never lead you astray. Call to Him and He will show you the hidden mysteries He wants you to spiritually see. He has secrets for you to discover and miracles for you to behold. Unwrap your gift from Jesus given to you because you have chosen the good portion.

Will you stay obedient to Jesus? He will manifest Himself to you when you keep loving Him. Show Jesus your love by keeping Him in the center of your life. Hold fast to your strong tower and your rock of refuge so He can fortify your faith in these uncertain times.

# September 23

*"When you see a cloud rising in the west you say at once; 'A shower is coming.' And so it happens."*
**Luke 12:54**

Jesus gives us signs in the heavens and on the earth for us to know what is to come. He shows us what He wants us to see so that we know He is with us. When a cloud rises in the west, we see that a shower is coming. We have seen these things before and we know they will happen again. But there are unseen things we cannot see but must believe by faith.

We know Jesus exists and we can trust Jesus in all situations even when we do not understand or cannot see. What things do you see happening around you that bring you hope for what is to come? Notice the love of God chasing the lost and reviving the hearts of people.

Keep praying for the lost to believe in God even before you see it with your eyes. Thank God in advance and let faith rise to believe what you hope for even before you see it happen.

# September 24

*"But I said to you that you have seen me and yet do not believe."*
*John 6:36*

Many will see and still not believe. Their hearts are hardened, and they cannot see how much they are loved. We cannot understand why these people have turned away from the truth. But what we do know is our Father loves us and wants us all to be saved by His grace. He touched our hearts and opened our souls when He made us new in Him and sealed us by the power of His love.

Why do you doubt God's love for you? You are worthy and valuable to God. He adores you and wants to see you abiding in Him and His love. God's love is unconditional and unmistakable. He is love, and whoever abides in love abides in God, and God abides in Him.

There is nothing that can separate you from the love of God in Christ Jesus. Your sins do not separate you from His love. He made you in His image and saw you even before you were born. He knitted you in your mother's womb. Receive this gift from the Father and open your heart to the redeeming love of Christ.

# *September 25*

*"Before the rooster crows today,*
*you will deny me three times."*
**Luke 22:61**

Jesus knew that His disciple, Peter, would deny Him three times. He told Peter that before the rooster crows, he would say that he did not know Jesus. He did not want to be seen as one of the followers of Jesus because he was afraid they would arrest him too. Instead of standing with Jesus, he turned away and denied knowing Jesus. We are people who fear when we do not totally trust the Lord to defend us. Jesus wants us to lay aside every fear.

Are you still carrying fear around because you have not fully trusted God to fight for you? He is waiting for your complete surrender to Him. He will take all you are carrying and make a way through your wilderness. There is nothing to fear but fear itself. Release the fear and you will be victorious!

Even though you walk through the valley of the shadow of death, fear no evil for God is with you. His rod and His staff will comfort you. He will lead you beside still waters and refresh your soul. He will make you lie down in green pastures. His goodness and mercy will follow you all the days of your life.

# September 26

*"I have said these things to you, that in me you may*
*have peace. In the world you will have tribulation.*
*But take heart; I have overcome the world."*
*John 16:33*

Jesus speaks His peace and life over us. He knows
what we will face in this world, but He also
knows His power will reign because He has
overcome the world! He defeated death and brought
new life. He rose from the grave so we could rise with
His love covering all our sins. He poured grace upon
grace over us so we could separate ourselves from the
world and be His beloved children. His love
conquered the grave, and His resurrection brought
new life to all who would believe. So, take heart, He
has overcome the world!

Do you feel His peace protecting your heart, soul, and
mind? When you are weak, God will be your
strength. He will remove all your worries and by His
presence give you perfect peace.

Close your eyes and let the peace of Jesus wash over
you right now. He knows what is troubling your heart
and wants you to release it to Him now. He will
rescue you from any issue you are dealing with in this
world.

# September 27

*"But now I am coming to you, and these things I speak in the world, that they may have my joy fulfilled in themselves."*
**John 17:13**

Jesus comes to us and speaks truth so that we will know we can have joy in Him. Joy is not found in our circumstances or successes, but in Him and our relationship with Him. We can have inner joy when Jesus is first in our lives. He wants us to make a place for Him in our hearts so He can fill us completely. He has come to live in us so that we may have joy and have it to the fullest!

Do you have joy? Think about how much Jesus has done for you and let His sacrifice of love touch your heart. For the joy set before Him, He endured the cross and overcame the shame just for you. He is now seated at the right hand of the throne of God interceding for you. Will you focus on the joy that is found in a relationship with Jesus?

No one can steal your joy when Jesus gives it to you. Nothing can take away the joy that He brings to your heart. Come to the joy of Jesus and let Jesus fill your cup until it overflows with His never-ending love!

# September 28

*"Father, into your hands I commit my spirit!"*
**Luke 23:46**

On the cross at calvary, Jesus called out these words in a loud voice and then He breathed His last breath. He had accomplished His mission on Earth, and it was time to go to the Father. He obeyed what He was to do so sinners could be saved! Redemption would be coming to His people! He would rise from the dead on the third day and the tomb would be empty!

The Son rose so you could be set free from the chains of sin. The stain of your sins were washed white by the power of the Lord. He committed His spirit so you could throw off the chains. Where the spirit of the Lord is, there is freedom!

Are you walking in freedom now that you are no longer bound up in chains? Jesus is always close to you and will never keep you buried in sin. He died so you could live. He conquered the grave so you could walk in victory. He rose so you could rise with Him. Let go of all the burdens you are carrying and surrender to the One who gave it all for you!

# *September 29*

*"I give them eternal life, and they will never perish, and no one will snatch them out of my hand."*
*John 10:28*

The gift of eternal life is for all who make Jesus their Lord! Jesus promises they will never perish, but will live forever! We can be sure of this because Jesus is faithful and righteous. There is a place called heaven waiting for us where death is no more, and pain is not present. We will be able to spend eternity with our Lord and Savior. What a day it will be when we meet Jesus face to face!

Do you know you are saved if you believe in Jesus by recognizing your need for a Savior in your heart and confessing your sins to Jesus with your mouth? Tell Jesus you love Him and want Him to live in your heart, now and forever. Believe that He has forgiven you for your sins. Receive His spirit in your soul and you will become a new creation. He takes your old self and puts a new heart and a new spirit within you fully alive and awakened to His love.

If you have already been saved, thank Jesus for saving you and giving you His life. Begin this new day with a grateful heart for your countless blessings.

# *September 30*

*"For I tell you, none of those men who were invited
shall taste my banquet."*
*Luke 14:24*

J esus invites all to come to His heavenly banquet.
But there are some who are too busy with the
cares of the world that they have not had any
time for Jesus. They put other people before Jesus and
cannot love Him with all their heart, soul, and mind
like He commands us to do. They are double-minded
and cannot give Jesus the full devotion He wants us to
give Him. These such people were invited but chose
to follow their ways instead of Jesus. They will miss
the banquet when the bridegroom comes for His
bride.

Jesus wants you to sit at His table and partake of His
banquet. You are a special guest and will be treated as
royalty. You are a chosen race, a royal priesthood, a
holy nation, a people for His own possession, that you
may proclaim the excellencies of Him who called you
out of darkness into His marvelous light.

Do not let anything stand in your way. He has given
you an opportunity that may not come again. The
time is now, and the hour has come for you to humble
yourself before the mighty hand of God.

*I am*
# THE BREAD
## OF LIFE.
JOHN 6:48

# *October 1*

*"But you will receive power when the Holy Spirit has come upon you, and you will be my witnesses in Jerusalem and in all Judea and Samaria, and to the end of the earth."*
*Acts 1:8*

When Jesus appeared to His followers after His resurrection, He clothed them with power from the Holy Spirit. to help them go, tell, and make more disciples. Jesus gave them this spiritual gifting that would allow them to minister, heal, and teach all He had instructed them. What a miracle for these witnesses to have seen the risen Jesus and be filled with His power!

Did you know the same power living in Jesus lives in you? The resurrection power is real and will help you do extraordinary things for the kingdom of God.

How do you know if the Spirit of Truth is living in you? If you have asked Jesus to be your Lord and Savior, He has already made you His own and deposited the Holy Spirit in you. He will be active in you when you surrender your will to His. You do this by listening and obeying His voice. You will hear Him as you ask and as you listen.

# October 2

*"If it is my will that he remain until I come, what is that to you? You follow me!"*
*John 21:22*

Jesus told Peter to follow Him. He wanted Peter to fix his eyes on Him and quit worrying about what others were doing. In the same way, Jesus wants us to keep abiding in Him and following Him so He can lead us where we are to go.

Have you chosen to listen to Jesus or other people? Jesus needs you to come to Him and stop listening to the other voices that lead you down the wrong path. They want to distract you. But you know what Jesus is speaking to you. He is giving you His plan for your life so that you can live victoriously.

What do you think Jesus is asking you to do? Spend time with Him so He can share truth with you and give you encouragement. Walk with Him in the scriptures, so He can talk to you through the pages of the Bible and point you to the path He wants you to take. Pray to Him, so He can hear your requests and answer you in His timing. His heart is close to yours, so follow Him to the places He wants to take you.

# October 3

*"But if anyone walks in the night, he stumbles, because the light is not in him."*
*John 11:10*

The darkness will keep us from walking in the light. We will stumble if we do not look to Jesus who wants us to be walking with God, the Father of lights. Every good and perfect gift is from above, coming down from the Father of lights, with whom there is no variation or shadow. The light would not be possible without God who is the light. Jesus wants us to stay close to the Father who will enlighten us with His wisdom and knowledge.

Do you see the light penetrating all the dark places inside you? Only God can uncover those hidden things that have made it impossible for you to see Him more clearly. His light will shine through the darkened areas in your life.

Jesus is asking you to wait for Him to guide your steps so you can shine His light. There are people living in darkness. He will direct them to you when you let His light shine through you. He will never let you walk in darkness when you are with Him, so shine brightly. Jesus is the bright morning star sent to show you the way.

HE SPEAKS TO ME

# October 4

*"You are those who justify yourselves before men,*
*but God knows your hearts. For what is exalted*
*among men is an abomination in the sight of God."*
*Luke 16:15*

God wants us to seek validation from Him and not men. He knows our hearts and our intentions and will exalt those who humble themselves before Him. God opposes the proud and gives grace to the humble. He does not want us to be swayed by things that are exalted among men like human power or money, but instead seek to please Him in all we do. Money will never bring us the security that God the Father brings, so cling to Him.

What is your focus? Are you more concerned about how much money you have or your relationship with God? He sees your heart and knows your thoughts. He also sees your struggles. He will never leave you alone but will provide all you need. Pray for Him to fulfill your needs and watch God fill them in His timing.

Seek God while He is near. God, rich in mercy and justice, brings real promises of truth and life so you never have to walk in fear. Walk by the guidance of the Spirit.

# October 5

*"For I tell you I will not eat it until it is fulfilled in the kingdom of God."*
*Luke 22:16*

J esus loves us and will wait to eat the Passover meal in the kingdom of heaven until the time comes for the resurrection of all believers into eternal life. The disciples were trying to understand all Jesus told them in His last days on earth, but they didn't fully understand. He wanted to open their hearts to His truth: That He is the way the truth and the life.

Do you hear Jesus calling you to come to Him? He knows your needs and wants to bless you. He will help you persevere in what you are going through so you can know His strength. Carry your cross, not as a burden, but as a gift, so you can do His mighty work!

Are you still trying to understand all that Jesus is sharing with you? He has called you to Himself so you can grow in truth and knowledge of what He wants for you. He came so you can have an abundant life. He wants you to rest in Him. He is the vine, and you are the branches. Abide in the vine so He can fill you with SAP, *Spirit as Power*, so you can live with great joy!

# October 6

*"So is the one who lays up treasure for himself and
is not rich toward God."*
*Luke 12:21*

Jesus teaches us not to lay up treasure here on
Earth, but to lay up treasure in heaven so we can
be rich toward God. He wants us to come to Him
with all our heart, seeking his desires for our lives.
The heavenly treasures we seek will keep us close to
God. The treasures on earth will be destroyed, but our
treasures in heaven last forever.

Spiritual treasures centered in the love of God will
bring endless joy while earthly things are short-lived
and not fulfilling to your soul. You cannot keep close
to God when you are too distracted by your
possessions. These can become idols in your life.
Challenge yourself to spend more time with the
heavenly Father. Breathe in the Spirit of God so His
power will revive you and center your focus on things
above.

Do you need revival of your heart and your soul? God
sees you. Delight in Him and be filled with His never-
ending joy. This joy will be your treasure that never
tarnishes. For where your treasure is, there your heart
will be also.

# *October 7*

*"Stay dressed for action and keep your lamps burning."*
*Luke 12:35*

We are instructed to stay dressed for action and be ready to encounter the days ahead. We need to clothe ourselves with the armor of God to be protected from any spiritual attack. Our armor is the belt of truth, the breastplate of righteousness, the shoes of the gospel of peace, the shield of faith, the helmet of salvation, and the sword of the spirit. When we put this armor on, we can stand against the schemes of the enemy!

Are you armored up? God protects you when you are. He will never allow spiritual defeat when you are dressed and ready to go. Never fear the evil one but keep your lamps burning with the anointing oil that covers you. Let Him find you wearing your armor and covered in oil, so you are ready and strong in the Lord.

Jesus will come at an unexpected hour. Be filled with wisdom and bring extra oil for your lamps so you can greet your bridegroom in faith and humility when He returns for His bride. Be empowered with truth from the Word and power from the Holy Spirit.

# October 8

*"Truly, I say to you, all sins will be forgiven the children of man, and whatever blasphemies they utter."*
*Mark 3:28*

Jesus reminds us that God forgives our sins and whatever blasphemies we utter when we are His children. The blood of Jesus covers all our trespasses and our sins. God gives us grace and removes the stain of sin so we will be washed clean. He takes away the guilt and replaces it with grace. Quit focusing on past sins and start looking to the One who removes all of them!

What past sins still haunt you? Let go of them. Jesus promises to remove sin so you can live in new life with joy and peace. You no longer walk in guilt and shame because Jesus has set you free from the weight of sin. Pray you will repent and lay all these sins down at the feet of Jesus.

Freedom reigns when sin is removed from your life. You will no longer be weighted down but lifted by Jesus. He wants to show you what He can do. Strip off every weight and run your race that God has set before you with endurance and joy!

# October 9

*"Why do you ask me about what is good? There is only one who is good. If you would enter life, keep the commandments."*
*Matthew 19:17*

Jesus reminds us that He is good. We can follow Him by doing what is good, righteous, and just. There are many who may not enter the kingdom of heaven because they are not truly following Jesus. But as His faithful servants, we can reach many people by sharing hope with the faith He gave us and the commandments He wrote for us.

Do you have faith to complete the work He has given you? God has a specific job for you in His kingdom. Pray He will make it clear so you can press on to do the works created for you. You are His masterpiece created for good works all for God's glory. Do not let fear stop you. Keep your eye on the prize, Jesus Christ. He needs to see your faith and your works for His kingdom glory.

The King holds you in the palm of His hands. Even though the storm is surging around you, Jesus saves you from drowning because He has covered you by the wonder-working power of His blood. We are saved to be a witness of the goodness of God.

# October 10

*"Therefore pray earnestly to the Lord of the harvest
to send out laborers into his harvest."*
*Matthew 9:38*

Jesus needs laborers in His harvest. These laborers will help our Lord with planting seeds and watering them so they can grow to be fruitful and multiply. God is the real Farmer who will give the growth, expansion, and advancement. It is our job to continue to work in the harvest by planting and watering in His kingdom.

God wants to give you more peace, wisdom, spiritual discernment, and sensitivity, strength, influence, joy, faith, love, and favor. He promises you will receive His gifts if you do His kingdom work by co-laboring where He calls you. Where have you been called? Seek the will of God and spread His blessings wherever you go.

God's will is to increase and multiply blessings of growth for His people. He sees the work you are doing and is pleased with you. He knows you are giving out of the abundance in your life. He has given you so much to share so you can receive all He has promised you. Do not grow weary of doing good, for at the proper time you will reap if you do not give up.

# October 11

*"Again you have heard that it was said to those of old, 'You shall not swear falsely, but shall perform to the Lord what you have sworn.'"*
*Matthew 5:33*

Jesus teaches us that we should not swear an oath, including swearing by heaven or earth. Our *yes* or *no* should be enough and we do not have to add an oath by invoking God. All the promises of God have their *yes* in Him. He keeps His promises to us, so will we keep our faith? Say *yes* and find that the promises of God will be a beacon of hope in this world.

Do you need hope right now? God knows things are pulling you away from Him, but He will bring you closer. Cling to His promises and know He will help you see your future is bright with Him by your side. He carries truth and will give you another chance to grow when you ask Him for direction. Call upon the Lord and He will answer you.

What is your deepest need right now? Ask the Lord and He will help you. He knows what you need. Simply ask and then give it to God thanking Him for His peace. He will not leave you until He has done what He has promised!

# October 12

*"And besides all this, between us and you a great*
*chasm has been fixed, in order that those who would*
*pass from here to you may not be able, and none*
*may cross from there to us."*
*Luke 16:26*

Jesus is warning us to make our lives count while
we are alive. If we choose greed and neglect the
poor, when we die, we cannot go back and be a
better person. There is no chance for salvation after
death. Not everyone will go to heaven, only those
who choose to believe and are saved.

Will you make your life count while you are living on
Earth? There are many things you can do to help
those in need. People need the saving grace of Jesus,
and you can help them find the truth. There are many
who are still living in the dark and need to find the
light. While the darkness exists, you will need to
shine His light even brighter.

Jesus wants you to be saved and have eternal life with
Him in heaven. And behold, He is always with you,
to the end of the age. Jesus seeks to win the affection
of your heart and will pursue you relentlessly,
tenderly, and joyfully. Will you listen and let go so
you can be with Jesus forever?

# October 13

*"If you can! All things are possible for one who believes."*
*Mark 9:23*

Jesus wants to remind us that all things are possible when we believe! He wants to show us He can do the impossible and our job is to simply believe by trusting Him with our whole hearts. It is His will that we have great faith. He will test us at times, and we will have to wait so our faith can grow for His glory to shine through! When the faith He has given us rises, we will see incredible miracles that only come from the Messiah through the Father who loves us!

Do you have faith? Jesus will give you glorious faith when you trust Him with all your heart. He will help you rise above anything you are facing when you abide in Him. Pray you will release your concerns fully to Jesus so He can make your path straight.

Will you believe in faith so you can see the miracles He has for you? Depend on Jesus for every move you make. Apart from Jesus, you can do nothing. When you let go and surrender your will to His, He promises to cover you with His faith that moves mountains!

# October 14

*"Woman, what does this have to do with me?*
*My hour has not yet come."*
*John 2:4*

Jesus, attending a wedding in Cana with his disciples, was asked to help with a problem. While they were there, the wine ran out. Mary, the mother of Jesus, asked Him to help. He answered that His time had not yet come because He was not ready to reveal to everyone who He was, but He knew He could help the servants by turning water to wine. He performed His first miracle here so He could help the master of the feast escape embarrassment. We see proof of how compassionate Jesus is in all circumstances.

Do you have a problem you know Jesus can fix? Ask Him to help you with it. He can bring you peace through it when you trust Him to do it. Only Jesus knows what you are facing and how He can help you. He might just share it with you and not let anyone else know what He has done for you. Or He might do something for you that will be openly revealed to others so they will believe.

Keep asking for help and stay hopeful that Jesus will work things out for good as you keep loving Him.

# October 15

*"They will put you out of the synagogues. Indeed, the hour is coming when whoever kills you will think he is offering service to God."*
***John 16:2***

Jesus tells His followers that once they claim Jesus as Messiah, they will be called out of the synagogues. The hour is coming when all will be persecuted and even killed for following Jesus. Those who condemn believers will be insulting Jesus and whose who call Him Lord. We can expect to be criticized for being a Christian, but remember we are blessed by God when we are persecuted for the sake of Christ. Blessed are we who endure hardships and suffer because of our faith.

Where is Jesus calling you to speak boldly as one of His followers? He wants you to step out in faith and speak truth in love. Only Jesus can protect you from the criticism you will face. He will defend you before your critics and give you strength to rise above it all. He knows how much you love Him and He is pleased with your faithfulness.

Keep fighting the good fight of the faith and share love with those around you for the sake of Jesus Christ who lives in you.

# October 16

*"Feed my lambs."*
*John 21:15*

Jesus instructs us to feed His lambs. He is the Good Shepherd who is calling us to disciple His own who are new in the faith and need guidance and direction. We are all in need of a shepherd who makes us lie down in green pastures of joy and still waters of peace. Jesus is the One who brings us back to Him when we choose to follow Him. Once we do, we will know how and what to feed His lambs.

You can be sure of His love for you and the joy that is found in Him when you make Him Lord of your life. You will know His voice as you stay close to Him. If you stray off course, His voice will not be the one you hear. Keep your eyes fixed on Jesus so you will be able to hear how you can help those around you.

You will finally hear and see what your role is to be when Jesus is the focus in your heart. He knows what you are facing and how you need to trust Him more. He will use you in ways you never thought possible so that your faith will carry you to new opportunities to shine!

# October 17

*"Then if it should bear fruit next year, well and
good; but if not, you can cut it down."*
*Luke 13:9*

Jesus disciplines us because He loves us. He will
prune us by cutting off the old so that new
growth can occur. We must abide in Jesus so He
can bear much fruit in us. We will not grow weary in
doing good when we are connected to the vine. The
sap of the vine will flow through us giving us more
energy to live and work in unison with Jesus.

What work does Jesus need for you to do? Surrender
your heart to Him today and ask Him where He needs
you. He will direct you to ways you can bear more
fruit so that He will grow a garden of love in your
heart and you will be a fruit-bearer for Jesus. He is
the Master Gardener who will feed and water you
with His Word and His Spirit.

Go and bloom where He plants you. Do not think that
someone else will do what He has called you to do.
He needs you to spread His sweet aroma of joy so
that others can bloom beautifully as well. He will use
you to bring peace to impossible situations so hope
will grow a garden of love.

# *October 18*

**"How many loaves do you have?"**
**Mark 8:5**

Jesus asks us important questions so we pause and reflect on when we see a need. He wants us to look within to see how we can use what we already have to make a difference where we are living. We have all been given specific gifts from the variety of spiritual gifts. Jesus wants us to look at what we have that can be multiplied. Much more will be given when we have faith in the little things and trust Him more with what we do have.

When you are faithful with a few things, He will put you in charge of many things. Enter the joy of your master. Can you see the few things He has entrusted to you? Trust Jesus more instead of relying on just yourself to figure it all out. He will give you His grand plan and will multiply joy in your life and in those around you.

Are you frustrated with your plan and tired of trying to find a solution? Keep your eyes upon Jesus and look in His wonderful face of grace. He is ready to show you a path that will bring you peace and joy when the task is completed. Gaze upon Jesus and you will know which path to take to victory!

# October 19

*"All these evil things come from within,*
*and they defile a person."*
*Mark 7:23*

Jesus knows that whatever comes out of a person's mouth is what is in their heart. Because we are human, there are evil thoughts that can enter our hearts and defile us. When we let go of the commands of God, we can be influenced by the world and its ways. Lies become prevalent in us when Jesus is not fully present in all that we do. We must surrender our hearts to Jesus to be filled with the Spirit. He will reside in us to keep us on the path of life.

Are you devoted to Jesus and fulfilling His commands? He has brought you out of the storm so you can see His light shining through. His hand is upon you as His child. Keep Him close and let His love be the reminder of what is good in your life.

Speak from a place of love and truth, then good thoughts will fill your mind and heart. Jesus puts His perfect love within you so you can know you are worthy. He will give you more than you can ever dream or imagine when you listen and obey His voice. What do you hear Him speaking to you?

HE SPEAKS TO ME

# October 20

*"I am the bread of life."*
*John 6:48*

Jesus is our bread of life. When we feed on His Word, we will not be hungry. He is our spiritual food who brings us wisdom, knowledge, health, and healing. He gives us all we need to help us grow our faith until we are overflowing with gratitude. We are His and He will make us whole again. All we have needed, He has provided in His timing and His will.

What are you longing for? Ask and you shall receive so that your joy may be full again. He knows you well and wants to speak to your heart. He loves to see you filled up with His joy so keep Him close and He will fill you with His spiritual food. His portion is perfect. Taste and see that the Lord is so good!

Are you feasting on the bread of life? He has come to bring you life in abundance. He has given you a taste of His healing because you have trusted Him. There is more healing for you, dear child. Come to the bread of life and let Him fill you up. You will never want when He is your Lord and Savior. Your heart and flesh may fail, but the Lord is your strength and portion, forever and ever!

# October 21

*"Sanctify them in the truth; your word is truth."*
*John 17:17*

Jesus has always prayed to the Father on our behalf. He prayed we would be set apart for God's special use and purpose. He wants us to be consecrated in the truth because His word is truth. He will show us the way when we come to Him with all humility. Our job is to love Him with all our hearts so that He can fill us with holiness and purity to do what we know is honorable and righteous in His eyes. He is interceding for us right now!

Jesus is the Word and the Truth. When you believe in Him and surrender your will to Him, He will fill you with all head knowledge and heart knowledge. You will know Him through His Word and He will give you the Holy Spirit to live inside your heart. When you come to Him, He will carry you in the palm of His hand, loving and protecting you always.

What do you need to tell Jesus? Talk to Him and tell Him how much you love Him. He will lavish you with His grace and pour His love over you. He will guide you to all truth and give you His perfect peace. He is the One who will strengthen you. Let go and let Him build you up!

# October 22

*"For this people's heart has grown dull, and with
their ears they can barely hear, and their eyes they
have closed, lest they should see with their eyes and
hear with their ears and understand with their heart
and turn, and I would heal them."*
*Matthew 13:15*

Jesus speaks of people whose hearts have grown
dull. With their ears, they can barely hear. With
their eyes, they cannot see. With their heart, they
cannot understand because they have turned away
from Him and turned toward the world and its ways.
If we return to Him with all our heart, He will heal us.
Pray for people to come back to their first love, Jesus
Christ.

Has your heart grown cold? If so, would you pray that
you would come back to Jesus? He knows you love
Him but He has not heard from you in a while. Listen
as He is calling you to Him. He will hold you close if
you let go and let Him restore you.

Jesus will revive you again! In His presence there is
fullness of joy and pleasure. He will never leave or
forsake you. Let Him hold you up and give you the
rest you need. You are His beloved whom He
cherishes.

# October 23

*"Recover your sight; your faith has made you well."*
*Luke 18:42*

Jesus healed a blind beggar in Jericho during the last Passover. Jesus saw the faith of the man who could not see and gave him sight. After the healing, the man glorified God and the crowd praised God when they saw what had happened. In the same way, God sees our faith, and when we believe He will heal us, we will see healing that can only come from the hand of our Almighty God.

Have you ever seen a miracle healing from God? If so, praise Him now for that reminder of how miracles are still alive. If not, pray that God will show you one because you believe they still exist. God will show you miracles and will give you hope. What is impossible with man is possible with God. Nothing is too big for your God!

Tell God what you need and wait patiently for His response. Remember He wants the best for you and will help you. The miracle might just be the moment you believed and invited Jesus into your heart. Open your eyes, keep praying, and never forget what God has done in the past. He will surely do it again!

# *October 24*

*"As the living Father sent me, and I live because of the Father, so whoever feeds on me, he also will live because of me."*
*John 6:57*

Jesus wants us to spiritually feed on Him so that we can live. All other food will not satisfy. When we feed on His food, we will never hunger again. He makes all things new and brings health and wholeness to all with the touch of His healing hand. The living Father wants us to be made whole, so let us come to Him with our mouths wide open so that He can fill us with His word and truth!

Are you hungry to know more about Jesus? Let Him satisfy your hunger and your thirst with the food and water that Jesus gives to those who seek Him. He will never leave you hungry or thirsty again. His food and water will bring health and life to your weary body and soul. He knows what you need, so come and feast on what Jesus gives.

Have you found yourself feeling empty and wanting more in this life? Jesus has come to bring you more than you can ever hope or imagine when you trust Him as your Lord and Savior. He brings hope and light to any situation. He will fill your every need.

# *October 25*

*"Come here."*
**Mark 3:3**

J esus is calling us to Him. He sees us and knows
that we need a Savior to help us. He clears a path
for us to come closer to Him. Jesus loves us and
needs us to be willing to come close so that He can
give us His instructions. He sees our struggles and
wants to be our very present help in trouble. He
knows our victories and celebrates with us. There is
no room for fear when Jesus is with us!

What challenge are you facing right now? Have you
asked Jesus to help you? He will take whatever
burden you have and remove every obstacle so you
can press forward with endurance and confidence.
Pray you will throw off everything that hinders you
and give it to Jesus. You can run the race marked out
for you if you will keep your eyes fixed closely on
Jesus Christ.

Think about the most difficult situation you have ever
faced. Were you a Christ follower then? Without
Christ, we will sink. With Christ, we will persevere.
Keep Jesus close at all times, so He can give you the
courage you need to run swiftly.

# *October 26*

*"When the Son of man comes in his glory, and all the angels with him, then he will sit on his glorious throne."*
*Mark 25:31*

Jesus promises He will return for His believers. If we are His, we will be among those who will come home with Him where He will sit on His glorious throne. We can only imagine the day when the Son of man will come in His glory with all the angels with Him! This glorious day will come at a time when we do not expect it, so stay awake and be ready. What a glorious day that will be!

Think of those who have passed away before you that you cannot wait to see again. Did they make the decision to follow Jesus? If they were Jesus followers, you will see them again. What a wonderful promise of hope from Jesus for all His Believers.

Are you anticipating the day when you see Jesus coming in the clouds in all His glory? The bridegroom will come to get you, His bride, so you can feast at His heavenly banquet. He has a place for you at His table of grace. Come to the Son and join those who will be celebrating in heaven together forever!

# October 27

*"The one who sows the good seed*
*is the Son of Man."*
*Matthew 13:37*

Jesus sows the good seed by planting His Word in the soil of our hearts. He will grow our faith as we open our hearts to hear what He is telling us. He will give us instruction and encouragement when we listen with ears to hear. Read His Word and take time to hear what Jesus speaks to your heart. Every good and perfect gift is from above and for our instruction and growth.

Jesus sows good seeds for you to bloom where He plants you. Where has He planted you? Think about the opportunities you have to grow and make a difference where you are now. What you do with your time matters. He will prompt you through the Holy Spirit to do things for His kingdom.

Make a list of places where you can serve. Pray for God to give you courage to do what He calls you to do. Then challenge yourself to do it to the best of your ability. He will give you strength to follow Him wherever He leads you. Be strong and courageous, for the Lord your God will be with you wherever you go!

# *October 28*

*"Teaching them to observe all that I have
commanded you. And behold, I am with you always,
to the end of the age."*
*Matthew 28:20*

Jesus needs us to teach others to observe all He
has commanded us. We can lead by example
when we are obedient. He asks us not to be afraid
to speak up when necessary. Fear will move us away
from the truth, but He will move in the hearts of His
people and will bless those who keep His
commandments. He never leaves His people and is
with us until the end of the age.

There are children who need to be taught. There are
adults who need to be instructed. Will you teach and
lead by example? God will honor your efforts. Share
the good news of the gospel of Jesus Christ so others
will believe.

How can they believe in Him if they have never heard
about Him? Speak about how much Jesus means to
you and how He has changed you. Your faith will
bring someone closer to God. That is why you must
go and tell. Share your story of salvation. Someone is
waiting to hear from you!

# October 29

*"This kind cannot be driven out by anything but prayer."*
*Mark 9:29*

When the disciples of Jesus asked why they could not drive out some evil spirits in a person, He told them there are things that can only be driven out by prayer. He explained there are kinds that will need much prayer and even fasting to leave a person. We can be prayerful people who keep praying until the spirit leaves. Our prayers make a difference, and God will hear each prayer we pray.

When two of you agree on earth about anything you ask, it will be done for you by the Father in heaven. For where two or three are gathered in His name, He is there among them. Keep meeting for prayer and calling upon the name of the Lord. He hears all your prayers and will answer you in His will and in His timing.

Do you meet regularly with others to pray? God is there with you when you pray together. He needs His people to pray and call upon His name. Pray for His will to be done and praise Him for His answers to your prayers. Rejoice in hope, remain patient in tribulation, and stay constant in prayer!

HE SPEAKS TO ME

# *October 30*

**"You are not far from the kingdom of God."**
**Mark 12:34**

Jesus commends those who speak truth about loving the Lord our God with all of our heart, soul, and mind. He blesses those who follow this greatest commandment. When we love the Lord this way, we will want to love our neighbors as Jesus loves and will not be far from the kingdom of God. When we are close to God, we are close to His kingdom.

Do you love your God with all your heart, soul, and mind? He has loved you first and He loves you so much that He gave His only Son so you can be saved from sin. Greater love has no one than this, that someone lay down his life for his friends. Jesus sacrificed all for you because He has great love for you!

Is your love for Him full of devotion because He is first in your life? He sees your commitment and will honor your diligence to obedience. For this is the love of God, that you keep His commandments and show Him that you love Him with a devoted heart. He knows your works, labor, and patience and will reward the faithful whose hearts are close to God.

# October 31

*"The days are coming when you will desire to see one of the days of the Son of Man, and you will not see it."*
**Luke 17:22**

Jesus was fully God and fully human moving among the people He saw and ministered to with compassion and kindness. He represented the kingdom of God as He fulfilled what He was called to do. The kingdom of God came with Jesus' ministry. The kingdom was there in Jesus Himself and is here in Jesus Himself now. And He has given us the power of the Holy Spirit to live in each of us now so that we can live and walk with new life in this darkened world where evil exists.

Do you know how powerful the Spirit is that dwells within you? The Holy Spirit will give you new life and new strength and help you rise to greater heights. He will brighten your world with joy so you will be filled with the light of His love.

Do you love God? Nothing can ever separate you from His amazing love. God's love is always present with us in the trials, the adversities, the joys, and the triumphs.

RECEIVE THE

*Holy*

SPIRIT.

JOHN 20:22

# November 1

*"And I tell you, everyone who acknowledges me before men, the Son of Man also will acknowledge before the angels of God."*
**Luke 12:8**

Jesus wants us to acknowledge Him before men. He will acknowledge us before the angels of God when we proclaim that He is our Lord and Savior. He will reward those who keep Him close and honor Him in all they do. We need to share the hope that is within us as we proclaim His majesty. If we tell others how great our Lord is because He transformed us, they will want to know Jesus as their Lord and Savior.

Your Lord seeks to save the lost and will chase after them until they come to Him. He wants us all to pursue Him and have a saving relationship with Him. Only Jesus can make a difference and bring the lost home. You know how He has made your life full. Tell others about why you love Jesus and how He set you free so that they will want to pursue Jesus like you do.

Have you told anyone about your Jesus? Let others know that He wants to be their Lord and that He will receive them when they come to Him. All who call upon the name of the Lord will be saved!

HE SPEAKS TO ME

# November 2

*"Go and show yourselves to the priests."*
*Luke 17:14*

Jesus healed people who had leprosy and He cleansed them of their terrible skin disease. These people were rejected and alone because of their condition. Jesus made them whole again because He had compassion on them. They reached out in faith and wanted to be healed, and Jesus saw their faith and healed them. He instructed them to show themselves to the priests as was commanded in the law after He healed them. They had a responsibility to act after Jesus helped them.

Jesus wants you to listen and obey His commandments. You do not need to be anxious when Jesus is there. He is in every situation and will attend to every need, even those you do not know you need. What is on your heart? Seek the Lord so that He can answer your deepest cry.

When you seek the Lord with all your heart, you will find Him. Only Jesus will meet you where you are and fill up your soul with His peace. What has you worried and anxious? Give it to Jesus and His peace will take precedence over everything!

# November 3

*"But no one can enter a strong man's house and plunder his goods, unless he first binds the strong man. Then indeed he may plunder his house."*
***Mark 3:27***

Jesus knew He would have to bind the strong man first before He could save us. He was willing to sacrifice all so we could be delivered from evil. When we let Jesus in our hearts, we will be rescued from our sins because He already won the victory!

Do not let your heart be troubled or afraid because Jesus has set you free from your sins so you can experience life everlasting. He knew how much you needed Him, so He suffered so you could be whole again and live a joy-filled life with His Spirit living in you. He will take you away from evil as you come close to Him and choose to give Him your heart.

Will you make Him Lord of your life? He has been calling for you to surrender to Him. He can take away all the cares of the world that hinder you from knowing Him more. Cast all your burdens to Jesus and He will take each one from you and give you rest. He will be with you always when you trust Him with your whole heart and love Him with all that is within you!

# November 4

*"You do not know what you are asking. Are you able to drink the cup that I am to drink?"*
*Matthew 20:22*

We have no idea how much Jesus had to endure for us to be forgiven. He drank the cup given to Him by the Father so that we could be rescued from the sins that entangle us. Jesus willingly drank of it when it was time knowing the difficulty He would experience. He did it all for us! What a beautiful outpouring of love He gave to us!

Jesus loves you. He calls you worthy because you are His child of grace. He offers you this gift of grace, so take it and experience a new life in Christ. Your old self passes away and a new life grows within you. It is time to put on the new life that is yours because Jesus drank the cup for you.

Have you ever thought about how hard it was for Jesus? He knew it would be tough, but He also knew your life would be full if He did what was prophesied for Him to do. Close your eyes and picture what Jesus took on for you. Then thank Him for your new life of joy that you have been given because of His redeeming love that covered all your sins!

# November 5

*"I say to you, rise, pickup your bed, and go home."*
**Mark 2:11**

Jesus healed many people during His ministry on earth. He saw those who needed help and healed them. At times He would heal because of other people's faith so all could see the glory of God in the healing. He healed a paralytic who was brought to Jesus through the roof. This lame man needed forgiveness and the ability to walk. Jesus saw the faith of his friends, which touched Him so much, that He gave healing to the man because of their great faith in action.

Do you have faith in healing for other people? If so, keep praying and asking Jesus to heal them. Believe they *can* and *will* be healed and never forget to pray, in faith, asking for the miracle in the name of Jesus. He hears all your prayers. He sees your faith and will reward your faithful actions in His will and timing. Do not give up, but keep believing, and you just might see that wonderful miracle.

Think of a need someone you know who needs healing. Pray faithful prayers for them and be encouraged as you draw closer to Jesus through your deep conversations with Him!

# November 6

*"Thus, when you give to the needy, sound no trumpet before you, as the hypocrites do in the synagogues and in the streets, that they may be praised by others. Truly, I say to you, they have received their reward."*
*Matthew 6:2*

Jesus wants us to give from our hearts because we are impacted by what we see and know we can help where we are needed. He does not want us to be hypocritical about how we give to others. He also does not want us to help only to receive praise. Jesus loves when we choose to give from our heart because we choose to live like Jesus wants us to live. He knows it is far better to give than to receive.

Who needs you to reach them? Think and pray about some needs in your community and how you can reach them with acts of kindness and service. Jesus sees your heart. Ask for direction and listen for ways you can make a difference and be a light.

The light shines brightest in the darkest times. Trust Jesus always and He will act. Commit your way to Him and He will lead you where you need to go. Keep shining your light so others will see your good works and give praise to the Father of Lights!

# November 7

*"Truly, I say to you, this poor widow has put in more than all those who are contributing to the offering box."*
*Mark 12:43*

We can all be like the widow who put in all she owned to contribute to the poor and needy. She gave all she had in her offering to God because she trusted God to take care of her. She let go of her coins with joy instead of complaining about what she did not have. Are we like the rich who only give out of obligation, or are we like the woman who gave because she knew God would give back everything she needed?

Do you give out of abundance or out of what is left over? Think about your giving habits and then pray about what God is calling you to give. He will show you where your generosity is needed. There are people hurting, and you can be the person who shares what God has given you. Keep seeking God and He will make it clear what you can do.

Be a giver of your gifts, time, and money, and He will bless you in ways exceedingly more than you can ever imagine. Are you ready to give?

# November 8

*"This is the bread that came down from heaven, not like the bread the fathers ate, and died. Whoever feeds on this bread will live forever."*
*John 6:58*

Jesus explains the significance of the bread of life to a group of Jews. He states that He is the bread of life and whoever eats of Him will live forever, unlike the manna, the bread of the His ancestors. Those who ate the bread of the fathers died, but those who ate the bread that came down from heaven would live. We can live, if we choose Jesus and eat of His daily bread.

Jesus wants you to come to Him so He can feed you His food. His food is to do His will and to finish His work. It is written that man shall not live on bread alone, but on every word that comes from the mouth of God. If you work for food that never spoils but endures to eternal life, the Father will place his seal of approval on you.

Are you spending time feeding on the Word of God? He has blessings for you as you eat the bread that sustains and enriches your life. You will never be thirsty again when you drink of His living water. So whatever you do, do it all for the glory of God!

# November 9

*"I am praying for them. I am not praying for the world but for those whom you have given me, for they are yours."*
**John 17:9**

Jesus is praying for us because He loves us. We are so blessed that Jesus appeals to the Father on our behalf and continually prays for us. He will never leave or forsake us because we belong to the Father. His everlasting love is wide, long, deep, and high. His love never fails but endures forever!

Jesus prays and His presence provides everlasting hope to those He prays for. You can be sure that He is praying for you if you are one of His. It is so wonderful to know that you are bathed in the prayers of your Savior. He not only saved you, but He has set you free from worry and distress because He is your Lord and prays over you.

Did you know Jesus never stops praying for you? He has your name on His lips and speaks love over you to the Father. Just when you think He does not remember you, listen to His love comforting you. His intercession to the Father will bring peace to your heart. Keep Jesus close and it will be well with your soul.

# November 10

*"Saul, Saul, why are you persecuting me? It is hard
for you to kick against the goads."*
*Acts 26:14*

Jesus spoke to Saul when He was persecuting
Him. He knew that Saul had been speaking and
trying to turn people against Him. He was
leading the charge against Jesus. But, Jesus, rich in
mercy, wanted Saul to come to the Savior and
believe. He never gave up on Saul but kept pursuing
Him until He saw the light!

Do you know people who persecute Jesus and do not
believe? Jesus knows who they are as well and will
keep praying for them to know Him. He is rich in
mercy and grace and will never stop praying for their
salvation. He believes they will see the light, just like
Saul finally did. Will you pray for these people until
they believe?

They will not know Jesus unless someone tells them
about Him. They will not understand unless someone
teaches them. They will not feel loved unless
someone shows them His amazing love. They will not
be saved unless they find their Savior, Jesus Christ.
Will you be the person who reaches someone?

# November 11

*"You heard me say to you, 'I am going away, and I will come to you.' If you loved me, you would have rejoiced because I am going to the Father, for the Father is greater than I."*
*John 14:28*

Jesus told His disciples that He would be going away so they would be prepared when the time came for Him to go to the Father. He did not want their hearts to be troubled, but for them to know His peace. As followers of Jesus, we can be sure that He will be with us always. He never leaves those He loves!

Jesus is with you in the presence and power of the Holy Spirit. Rejoice, for the Lord is with you in whatever you do. He will take you to places you never thought possible. He will bring you through things that help you see Him more fully. Keep your faith alive and you will rise to great heights with Jesus.

If you are struggling, Jesus wants you to ask Him for help. He will move the mountain you are facing if you keep your faith alive. You never have to worry when Jesus is with you. Let go of the worry once and for all and watch your mountain move!

# November 12

*"But the tax collector, standing far off, would not even lift his eyes to heaven, but beat his breast, saying, 'God, be merciful to me, a sinner!'"*
*Luke 18:13*

We are all sinners in need of a Savior. Jesus came so all of us could receive mercy and grace. Once we realize how we need to be saved, we can come to the Father just as we are and repent of all our sins. He will take all our sins and wipe every one of them away if we will humble ourselves before Him. God will be merciful and cover us with grace because He loves us.

Come close and recognize your need for a Savior. Confess and believe in your heart and Jesus will make you one of His own. He has been waiting for you and those you love to come while there is still time. He will come again for His bride and wants you to be able to feast with Him at His heavenly banquet.

Do you Hear His still, small voice calling you closer to Him? He is not disappointed in you but is ready to receive you into His kingdom. Make this decision to follow Him and you will never walk alone. Receive Jesus Christ in your life and live forever!

# November 13

*"I thank you, Father, Lord of heaven and earth,*
*that you have hidden these things from the wise and*
*understanding and revealed them to little children."*
**Matthew 11:25**

Little children are special to Jesus. He wants children to come to Him because they have the faith Jesus wants in all of us. Children trust Jesus without having to understand all the details. They see His love and they openly receive it with humility and excitement. Children are a gift from God, for the kingdom of God belongs to them. Unless we turn to Jesus and become like these little children, we will never enter the kingdom of God.

Have you seen the love a child has for Jesus? Children have been given the gift of faith from the Lord of Heaven and Earth. As they grow, children need to be taught more about Jesus and their need to keep Him close to their hearts.

If you teach children about Jesus, when they are old, they will not depart from Him. Jesus wants them to confess their need for a Savior and decide to ask Him into their hearts. Will you share the good news of the gospel with the children in your life?

# November 14

*"And you shall love the Lord your God with all your heart and with all your soul and with all your mind and with all your strength."*
*Mark 12:30*

Jesus taught us to love the Lord our God with all our heart, soul, mind, and strength. This commandment is the greatest because without our love for Him being first in our life, we will love ourselves or other people more and cannot live the way He wants us to live. Our love for Him should come before anyone or anything else.

Do you love the Lord with all your heart, soul, mind, and strength? If you are not sure, ask yourself who is most important in your life and what or who you think about most of the time. If your answer is Jesus and you can honestly say that you are devoted to Him, then you have followed this greatest commandment. If you are not sure, pray you will love the Lord first and let go of other things that keep you from Him.

Jesus wants your total devotion. Joy and peace will flood your soul when you surrender to Him. Fall in love with Jesus Christ!

# November 15

*"I am the living bread that came down from heaven.
If anyone eats of this bread, he will live forever. And
the bread that I will give for the life of the world is
my flesh."*
*John 6:51*

Jesus came down from heaven as the living bread
for us to eat so that we will live with Him
forever. He gave the bread of life by giving of
His flesh. He suffered for our sake so we could be
with Him in the kingdom of God. He came so we
could have life and have it everlasting. We have been
given a gift to open and eat so we will live with Him.
Taste and eat while the time is still here. He is coming
for His bride soon!

Imagine all Jesus suffered for your sake and pray that
you will remember this as you commune with Him at
His table where He has welcomed you. Remember all
that Jesus did for you and pray that you would
remember His sacrifice every time you take
communion.

Jesus knew you would need a Savior because sin
came into the world. He endured the pain so you
could rise with Him. He did everything as the Father
commanded so that you could be with Him forever!

# November 16

*"Daughters of Jerusalem, do not weep for me, but weep for yourselves and for your children."*
*Luke 23:28*

Jesus tells a group of women on the Via Dolorosa not to weep for Him but for themselves and their children. He warned that a day would be coming when those who are childless will be blessed because of the tribulation that all of us and our children would face someday. God would allow this tribulation to come into their lives to test and strengthen their faith. He allows these things so we will grow our faith and come closer to Christ.

What are you trying to do all by yourself without fully trusting God? Whatever it is, let it go, and trust God. He wants to bless you but requires you to commit to Him. Those who seek after God will be richly blessed by the Lord who gives greater faith to those who have a close relationship with Him.

Will you keep seeking more of your Lord so He can strengthen your faith? There are countless ways you can get to know Him better. It begins with a surrendered heart close to His. Keep searching for Him while He is near so He will speak truth to you.

# November 17

*"I in them and you in me, that they may become perfectly one, so that the world may know that you sent me and loved them even as you loved me."*
**John 17:23**

Jesus prays for all of us to be one as He and the Father are one. He wants us to know that the Father sent Him as the Savior because He loved us so much. Jesus died so we could be free from the sins that bind us. Jesus wants to set us free from sin by breaking the chains that imprison us. He will keep praying for us until we let go and are free at last.

Are you pressing forward with Jesus or pulling away from Him? He prays for you to open your eyes to His call upon your life. He wants you to be united with other believers so that together you can work for His glory. He hopes you will spread the gospel of peace and press on in the faith.

You are predestined, called, justified, and glorified to work for His kingdom's purposes. He will equip you to do every good work until He completes the work He has for you. Pray for revelation to hear what He is speaking to you and then accomplish the task at hand. He will be a very present help if trouble comes. Be a brave soldier for Christ!

# *November 18*

*"When you pray, say: "Father, hallowed be your name. Your kingdom come."*
*Luke 11:2*

Jesus teaches that when we pray, we need to say that our Father's name is hallowed. God's name and God Himself should be the most valued thing in our life and in our world. His name is holy as He is holy, and when we pray, we need to reorient our lives around Him and His will for us on Earth. His name represents His character as Father, Son, and Holy Spirit. We can pray for His kingdom to come to Earth as it is in heaven and then work so He is honored and glorified.

When you pray, God hears your prayers for His people, and He listens with love. Those who fear the Lord and obey His commandments will be rewarded and renewed. Trust and obey so that you will hear His will for you.

You are close to God when you pray. Your relationship with Him will grow when prayer is a part of your life. He is listening to you as you talk to Him. He wants deeper conversations with you and enjoys hearing your requests. Keep praying and stay alert!

# November 19

*"They will pick up serpents with their hands; and if they drink any deadly poison, it will not hurt them; they will lay their hands on the sick, and they will recover."*
**Mark 16:18**

Jesus reassured His disciples they would do greater things than He did. It is hard to understand how they would be able to pick up serpents with their hands and be able to drink deadly poison and it not hurt them. But Jesus covered and anointed them with power to overcome evil and heal the sick. As disciples of Jesus, we can also do greater things. Wake up and follow His promptings without delay.

You have been given power from Jesus to overcome evil and spread joy and kindness. He will put people in your path who need His light in their lives. He needs you to use your voice to share the gospel of peace and your hands and feet to love those who need to know Jesus as Lord.

Jesus Christ is the same yesterday, today, and always. His light glows for all. Look up into the night skies and see the stars shining to remind you how the love of Jesus shines brightly for you.

# November 20

*"For as the lightning flashes and lights up the sky from one side to the other, so will the Son of Man be in his day."*
*Luke 17:24*

Storms bring lightning to light up the sky from one side to the other. When we see this wonder, we watch in awe of what the Father can do. Jesus will return in His glory with the brightest light we have ever seen covering the earth. We will see the darkness turn to light in the blink of an eye. Those who follow Jesus will go with Him into the light. What a day that will be!

Do you wonder what it will be like when Jesus returns for His own? There will be many left behind who rejected the Son of Man. Those He brings home will experience what He has promised and will be overwhelmed with what they see. Be sure of your salvation before He comes back to retrieve those who are His.

Remember when you accepted Jesus into your heart? Praise Him for this glorious transformation! If you are not sure if you are saved, be sure today, by telling Jesus you believe He is Lord. Confess your sins to Him, repent, and He will forgive you.

# November 21

*"If I had told you earthly things and you do not believe, how can you believe if I tell you heavenly things?"*
*John 3:12*

Jesus wants us all to believe, but unfortunately there will be many who do not believe. He knew many people did not even believe the earthly things that Jesus told them when He ministered to the crowds. They questioned and even challenged His teachings and authority. He knew there would be more who could not believe the heavenly things He shared with them. Only those who believe can be saved.

Do you believe? Jesus shares truth with you and wants to see your faith. Why are you questioning? He has given His life as proof of His love for you. Through his resurrection He conquered death to defeat the enemy and show you what a marvelous Savior He is!

If questions still arise in your heart, ask Jesus to show you and reveal these mysteries to you. He will show you great and wonderful things when you love and obey Him. Believe in the impossible and know there are miracles waiting for you.

# November 22

*"Do not marvel that I said to you,*
*'You must be born again.'"*
*John 3:7*

We wonder how we can be with Jesus when he sits at the right hand of the throne of God. We cannot see Him with our eyes, but by our faith, we believe He is with us. His Spirit dwells within us if we are born again into His kingdom. He saves all who call Him Lord. He will keep trying to reach us until we are found.

Jesus has come to seek and save the lost. He needs you to share the good news of the gospel. Who will you tell today? If you do not share, how will they know the truth?

Who do you know that is not born again? Pray for them to make this decision because time is of the essence for all to believe. The days are drawing closer, and the opportunities are diminishing for people to come to the Savior before the great day of His coming. He is waiting until the time the Father sends Him to collect His bride, and you do not know the hour or the day. Only the Father knows, so share truth with those He sends to you so that they will be saved!

# November 23

*"Father, glorify your name."*
**John 12:28**

Jesus asked for the Father to glorify His name to the people. After He prayed this prayer, the Father answered from heaven that He had both glorified it and would glorify it again. The Father said that He glorified His own name through the life of Jesus and would glorify it again when Jesus died on the cross and was resurrected from death to life. Jesus prayed and the Father answered Him. He wants us to model His example of fervent prayer and keep close to Him as we pray.

When you pray, there is an intimacy that develops between you and Jesus. He takes your prayers to the Father who hears and answers in His will and His timing. There is never a prayer that is not heard. Your Heavenly Father wants to hear you pray. Jesus loves to intercede for you. The Holy Spirit will give you the words to say when you do not know what or how to pray. Commit to pray more and your relationship will grow deeper.

The Father is waiting for you. He listens with love and grace. He will comfort you and give you peace to cover all your burdens. Let Him unburden you!

# November 24

*"Receive the Holy Spirit."*
*John 20:22*

J esus spoke these beautiful words when He came back after the resurrection to appear before His disciples in the upper room. Jesus breathed the life-giving gift of the promised Holy Spirit who would live and move in His believers. He will give us the same power that raised Him from the dead when we believe and look to Him for our strength and purpose. He wants all to receive the Holy Spirit.

Will you receive this wonderful gift from Jesus? He will seal you with the Holy Spirit when you make the choice to believe. Jesus will never stop depositing peace in you when you let Him work in and through you. Step aside and surrender so He can give you strength for the road ahead. He will give you new spiritual life that will enrich you in every way,

The Holy Spirit will prompt you to do what Jesus needs you to do. He will never lead you astray or in the wrong way. He only has His best planned for you, so go where He directs you. With the strength and the direction of the Holy Spirit, you will be able to do exceedingly more than you could before He deposited His Spirit in you!

# November 25

*"Children, do you have any fish?"*
***John 21:5***

Jesus asks His children if they have any fish because He sees they have not caught any. He knows the answer to the question will be *no* and He wants to direct them to the area where the fish are plentiful. The disciples did not recognize Jesus at first when He asked the question, but later they see it is their Savior coming to help them. He continues to care for His disciples and will always help them find what is necessary. He will bring supernatural blessings when we stay obedient to Him.

Have you been looking for the blessings of Jesus or are you still focused on the problems surrounding you? If you ask, Jesus will show you how you can live with His spiritual blessings. He wants to give life in abundance but is waiting for you to admit you need Him in your life. He will give you what you need.

He is calling you to feed His sheep and shepherd those He puts in your path. He will give you more spiritual blessings when you trust Him with all that is within you and step into your destiny without fear and worry. It is time to stop just trying and start trusting!

# *November 26*

*"Take care, and be on your guard against all covetousness, for one's life does not consist in the abundance of his possessions."*
*Luke 12:15*

Jesus knows people will covet things that others have if their focus is just on earthly possessions. When we idolize material items, God cannot be first place in our life. Jesus warns us to take care and be on our guard against an excessive desire to have something that belongs to someone else or possess more than we need. He knows that if we are covetous, we will never be satisfied.

Let Jesus satisfy you with His spiritual blessings. There are blessings waiting for you and opportunities for you to grow closer to Him. You do not need to be envious or jealous of what others have. You have been given exactly what will make your life full because you have a relationship with Jesus.

Write down all your blessings and thank Jesus for giving you exactly what He knows will bring joy to your life. All those other things look good on the outside but will leave you feeling empty on the inside. Contentment begins and ends with Jesus Christ. Things can never fill you, but Jesus can!

# November 27

*"Heaven and earth will pass away,*
*but my words will not pass away."*
*Mark 13:31*

The words of Jesus will remain forever. His words are true and not relative to time, place, or culture. His promises will be fulfilled, and His words will guide us to all truth. Even if heaven and Earth pass away, Jesus and His words will live forever. We can count on Him in all ways and in all circumstances. He is the best *yes* we will ever say and the greatest Savior we could ever have.

Will you trust and believe what He is speaking to you? His treasures of truth will bring joy to your heart. You have left your first love because you are setting your mind on the things of this earth. Set your mind on the things above where moths and dust cannot destroy. Heaven's treasures are so close that you can touch them when you speak Jesus over your life.

Have you been reading and studying the Word? God has given you commands so you can be well-equipped for what is to come. He will show you the way if you ask and let Him lead you to greater works that He wants to do in you.

# November 28

*"To proclaim the year of the Lord's favor."*
*Luke 4:19*

The Lord will pour His favor over us when we stay obedient to His commands and commit our plans to Him. The favor of God touches those who proclaim His righteousness and live holy and pure lives devoted to Christ. We can live this way when our hearts are connected to His and our minds are focused on how God wants us to live. When we give Him glory and seek to serve Him in all that we do, He is well pleased with us.

Do you see the favor of God in your life? If so, He is well pleased with you and is blessing your actions and attitudes. He will give you the desires of your heart when you delight in Him and seek His will. Instead of asking why, He wants you to ask for His guidance and use every good gift He has given you.

What gifts have you been given to bless others for God's glory? If you do not know what spiritual gifts you have, ask God to show you. Every good and perfect gift comes from the Father. Pray for wisdom and knowledge about how and where you can use your special gifts and use them for His glory!

# November 29

*"The harvest is plentiful, but the laborers are few."*
**Matthew 9:37**

Jesus needs workers now, for the harvest is plentiful and the laborers are few. There is so much work left to do, and He knows He can count on those of us whose hearts are close to Him. Start faithfully praying for the laborers to fill the needs of the people who are searching for hope. Give as God leads and serve as God directs. It will take all of us to make a difference for His kingdom work. Ask others to join Him in the work He is already doing.

Where do you see God at work around you? He is showing you places you can serve and people you can minister to right now. There are people who need the love of Jesus and are searching for the wrong things. You can be that one person who could bring them back to Him. Pray for the light to shine on their sins so they will ask for forgiveness.

Do you know people who might be willing and able to work with you to spread the good news? If so, begin asking them and make every effort to supplement your faith with good works. God will reward your faithfulness as you see lives changing one by one.

# November 30

*"Go away, for the girl is not dead but sleeping."*
*Matthew 9:24*

Jesus had the power to raise the dead to life. He gave new life to those who were physically dead and spiritually dead. Even when others did not believe, He showed up and brought miracle healings where they were needed. Jesus has given us the power to pray over people to be healed. He will still heal now just as He did before. There are miracles waiting to be revealed in this day and time.

Do you believe in miracles? They are just as relevant today. Pray that Jesus will show you a miracle He desires for you to see. Think about your salvation experience. That is a miracle right there. The day you asked Jesus into your heart gave you spiritual healing. What about the birth of a baby? That is the miracle of life from your heavenly Father just for you to experience.

God knitted you in your mother's womb and handcrafted every part of you. Have you ever thought about the fact that you are God's miracle? Thank Him for creating the miracle of life for you as He made you in His image out of His love!

Let your hearts
not be troubled.
*Believe in God;*
BELIEVE ALSO
*in Me.*

JOHN 14:1

# December 1

*"Have you not read this Scripture: 'The stone that the builders rejected has become the cornerstone.'"*
*Mark 12:10*

Jesus was denied and scorned by those who came against Him. The Jewish leadership rejected Jesus the same way builders reject the cornerstone on which all buildings depend. They did not accept Jesus as the chief foundation stone of the church. We also can be people who rebuke the Messiah by our thoughts and our actions that come against Him. God sees this and it saddens Him that we act this way. He wants our full surrender because He is the cornerstone and the foundation of the church. Jesus is the way, the truth, and the life. No one comes to the Father except through Him!

Are you rejecting Jesus by your words or your deeds? Examine your heart to see if you are in the faith. Test yourself to see if you are truly a believer in Jesus Christ. See if you are in line with the truth of the gospel of Jesus by your actions and obedience. He wants all your heart so He can do something new in you.

Will you give Him you whole heart? Call upon your Savior and lean on Him so that He can be your Rock.

# December 2

*"Behold, I am sending you out as sheep in the midst of wolves, so be wise as serpents and innocent as doves."*
*Matthew 10:16*

Jesus sends us out as sheep in the midst of wolves. But He is our Good Shepherd who will guard and protect us from those who try to harm us. When anyone tries to come against us, we have the full armor of God to cover us. We also have the sword of the Spirit and prayer to communicate with God so we can hear His voice guiding us into all truth and strengthening us for the battle ahead.

Are you using the wisdom God has given you to detect those who want to come against you and your Savior? Be wise as serpents and innocent as doves when you go out to see those who will betray you. Ask for the Holy Spirit to show you the truth and give you discernment of good and evil.

Use the armor you have been given for battle. God has given you the belt of truth, the breastplate of righteousness, the shield of faith, the helmet of salvation, the shoes of peace, and the sword the of the Spirit. Put these on and you will be victorious against any enemy you will encounter.

# December 3

*"Do not be afraid; go and tell my brothers to go to
Galilee, and there they will see me."*
*Matthew 28:10*

After the resurrection, Jesus revealed Himself
alive to a few women and told them to go and
share the good news with His brothers. These
women humbly fell at His feet and worshipped Him.
He knew they would go and tell the disciples the
wonderful news that He was alive and would see
them again in Galilee.

Can you imagine how marvelous it was for those
women to see Jesus again in His resurrected body?
He accomplished what was promised and came to
fulfill the ministry He was called to do. God was able
to do exactly what He said He would do, and the
women rejoiced together for what came to be.

Will you rejoice knowing that what you hope for will
come true? Jesus Christ came to love you as one of
His own. He loved you so much that He promised to
bring you life everlasting. He will never leave you but
will stay with you wherever you go. Why are you still
afraid of bad news? Let it go and surrender all your
worries to the Prince of Peace.

# December 4

*"But I say to you, Love your enemies and pray for those who persecute you."*
*Matthew 5:44*

Many people think it is right to dislike their enemies and turn against them. The world tells us to be offended when someone does not agree with our way of thinking. But Jesus tells us to love our enemies and pray for those who persecute us so we can live as kingdom people with love in our hearts. If we follow Jesus, we will show love to our enemies.

If people come against you, would you stop and pray for them like Jesus instructs you to do? It seems upside down to love someone who does not treat you with love and respect, but when you do, you honor Jesus. He gave His life to give you love. Now it is your turn to give your love, even to those who may not love you back.

Pray about ways you can show love to the unlovable. You cannot control their behavior toward you, but you can control the way you treat them. Try being kind to your offender and forgiving them in your heart. Do not be overcome by evil, but overcome evil with good.

# December 5

*"O you of little faith, why did you doubt?"*
*Matthew 14:31*

Our faith is important to Jesus. He wants us to stop doubting and start trusting Him again. Just when we think we cannot go a step farther, He will give us courage to go the extra mile and faith to step forward even when we do not see all the details. Our doubt will be defeated when Jesus is the foundation of our faith. We can trust Him with all our heart and soul when we make Him our friend.

Jesus knows you have been questioning some things in your life. He wants you to see the beauty of what He has planted in your life and not focus on the things you cannot change. Have you noticed the blessings He has put in your life despite the difficulties? Open your heart and stop doubting and start trusting again to see what He wants to show you.

Will you keep Jesus close to your heart? All those things that have pulled you away from Him are not important. Trust your Wonderful Counselor with all that is within you, and He will give you a faith that moves mountains. Forget what lies behind and press on to what lies ahead, your prize, Jesus Christ.

# December 6

*"Come away by yourselves to a desolate place*
*and rest a while."*
**Mark 6:31**

J esus calls us to come to a desolate place by ourselves and rest for a while. He knows our bodies need rest so He asks us to come to Him to find our rest. He will take our burdens, so we do not have to walk alone. Jesus loves to see us take off all that weighs us down so He can lift us up.

What is weighing you down? Take off what holds you back and yoke yourself to Jesus. He will be with you every step of your journey when you are close to Him. Those temptations you are facing are opportunities for you to grow your faith when you let Jesus provide a way out of your stress and give you rest.

Jesus will answer all your requests with His love and grace. He is the answer to all your questions. Pray that you will stop trying to figure it out by yourself and let Him show you the way. He has a better plan and will provide another way. Quit going back and start moving forward. He will rewrite your story of shame and turn it into a story of victory!

# December 7

*"In the same way, let your light shine before others,
so that they may see your good works and give glory
to your Father who is in heaven."*
*Matthew 5:16*

Jesus sees the light we are shining before others so they may see our good works and give glory to our Father who is in heaven. He knows our world is dark and that His light can make all things bright. His Word is a lamp to our feet and a light on our path. When we listen and obey what He is telling us through His living Word, we will see with spiritual eyes.

Are you shining His light before others through your works and by your faith? People will remember how you made them feel even if they do not remember what you said. Be one who brings blessing and not cursing. Seek truth and Jesus will light your path.

Are the words of your mouth and the mediations of your heart pleasing to the Lord? If you are not sure, ask the Lord to show you where your hardened heart needs to be softened. He will remove your heart of stone and replace it with a heart of flesh so you can do the good works He has prepared for you. Be a light!

# December 8

*"If anyone has ears to hear, let him hear."*
*Mark 4:23*

Jesus wants us to hear Him speak to us. He has specific things to tell us if we will open our ears to hear. There are people who are too interested in what *they* are saying that they fail to hear Jesus calling them to a saving relationship with Him. Selfishness takes over and they hear only the things that interest them. Do not be one of these who fail to listen but be a part of the family of God who have faith to see and ears to hear His voice of truth and grace.

Do you hear what the Lord is speaking to you? He speaks truth in the Spirit so you can discern good from evil. He has shared His Word with you. With the Spirit and the Word active in you, revival will happen in your heart, and Jesus will do mighty things in and through you.

Keep your ears open and your heart ready to receive what Jesus has for you. His peace will inhabit your prayers and your praises, and His joy will make His home in you. With all His peace and joy living in you, all hope will invade any negative thought, and your faith will explode like never before!

HE SPEAKS TO ME

# *December 9*

*"You must also be ready, for the Son of Man is coming at an hour you do not expect."*
*Luke 12:40*

Our world is constantly changing and this change can certainly be difficult. But we can be sure that Jesus will never change and will be constant and consistent in our lives when we make Him our Lord and Savior. He will bring us through anything we face when we choose Him. We must also be ready for Jesus will return and come at an hour that we do not expect. What a glorious day that will be for all His Believers!

Are you ready? If you are, there is no need to worry about when He will return because you will be with Him forever. You are His because you belong to the kingdom of God. If you are not ready and do not know Him as your Lord, you will miss out on Him coming to take His bride and you will be left behind with regret and pain and so much weeping and gnashing of teeth. Those who are left will wish they had been ready for the Son of Man.

It is time to help all those you know to come to Jesus. He is ready to receive all who believe in Him and desire to make Him Lord.

# December 10

*"For everyone who asks receives, and to the one who seeks finds, and to the one who knocks it will be opened."*
*Matthew 7:8*

Ask, seek, and knock and the door will be opened by Jesus. For everyone who asks Him for what is on their heart by seeking Him with all their heart will find Him. Keep knocking so He can open the door. The greatest gift of His Spirit will be ours as we continue asking, seeking, and knocking. He gives much as we give Him our hearts and are intentional with our actions of love for Jesus.

Where can you start seeking Him more? Stay faithful and He will open the door wide for you. Only God will close the door if He needs you to switch directions and open different doors. He has plans laid out for you, so trust Him to help you see what He needs you to see.

Are you having trouble knowing the direction He has laid out for you because of all the decisions you are trying to make alone? Keep praying and leaning on Jesus and He will reveal all He is trying to tell you. Only Jesus can give you the right choice when you ask, seek, and knock.

# December 11

*"Father, if you are willing, remove this cup from me. Nevertheless, not my will, but yours, be done."*
Luke 22:42

Jesus asked the Father to remove the cup He knew He must drink as He poured out His heart to Him in prayer. He pleaded for mercy knowing His Father could change His mind if it was His will. But Jesus, full of love for us and devotion for His Father, was willing to drink the cup for all of us to be free from sin. He would be obedient if the Father willed it to be done. Jesus knew the suffering He must endure for all to be saved would lead us to have life everlasting and transformed hearts.

Is there something God has asked you to do that you know is His will for you, but you have let fear stop you? When your heart follows Him, He will replace fear with courage and strength. What seemed so difficult in the past will be easy to do when you remember what Jesus did for you!

The risk is far worth the reward when you step out of your comfort zone. Because with Jesus, nothing can stop you. He will remove obstacles that seemed impossible to move and will give you needed faith to do the work.

# December 12

*"And everyone who hears these words of mine and does not do them will be like a foolish man who built his house on the sand."*
*Matthew 7:26*

Jesus warns us to listen to what He says so we will not act like a foolish man who built his house on sinking sand. Without the guidance of Jesus, we will sink, but with His truth as our cornerstone we will be able to stand firm. Jesus has given each of us specific gifts so we can do what we have been predestined to do.

Set your sights on Jesus and His plan for your life. His blueprint for your life will help you construct what He needs you to build for others to grow. Pray you would be still and spend more time with Jesus.

Have you given Jesus at least five minutes of your time each day by reading your Bible every day? When you spend this time with Him, you will hear His voice and the scriptures will come to life. The Word of God is active and alive. He has breathed life into every word. Open your mouth so He can fill it with truth. For what comes out of the mouth, is what is written on your heart. Be sure that your mouth proclaims the glory of Jesus!

# December 13

*"Was it not necessary that the Christ should suffer these things and enter into his glory?"*
**Luke 24:26**

Jesus Christ suffered the things that were preordained for Him so He could be resurrected to life! Without His death and resurrection, we would not have forgiveness from sin and everlasting life. We also would not be able to have a relationship with the Father that is only possible through His Son. He came so we could know the Father, the Son, and the Holy Spirit intimately. They are one so we can be one with them.

When we give our hearts to Jesus, He takes residence in our hearts, minds, and our souls, forever. We can grow our relationship with Him through our obedience and our trust. With the Father above us, Jesus beside us, and the Holy Spirit inside of us, nothing can stop us from pursuing our higher calling!

What is your higher calling? Once you seek Him with all your heart, you will begin hearing His voice and seeing manifestations of His glory in and around you. Look around you and see what Jesus is revealing to you.

# December 14

**"Peace to you!"**
**Luke 24:36**

Jesus was born to bring peace to all the world. For onto us a child was born and to us a Son was given! His birth was peaceful and filled with promise for a Savior was born for all of us. His birth was anticipated by all and received by many. But there were still some who did not believe Jesus was born to be our Wonderful Counselor, Mighty God, Everlasting Father, or the Prince of Peace. Those who did believe knew Jesus was the Messiah who fulfilled the promise of a peace that would have no end.

Will you receive His peace? Jesus is proclaiming peace over you and your family. He is your Prince of Peace calling you to lay down your burdens and strife and come to Him fully surrendered. He has overcome the world just for you!

Take a moment and picture the night Jesus was born. Imagine if you were there among the shepherds who heard the singing of the angels and the proclamation of the long-awaited Messiah. Rejoice with the angels and sing praise for the King who has come to live in your heart! He has accomplished what He set out to do through His birth and His resurrected life.

# December 15

*"And if I go and prepare a place for you, I will come again and will take you to myself, that where I am you may be also."*
*John 14:3*

W e can be sure that when we pass from this life as a Believer in Christ, that Jesus will bring us to the place He has prepared for us. He will come again to take us to Himself so where He is, we will be there also. What a promise we can cling to when life on Earth gets difficult! There is no fear in death, but there is hope for what is to come. Focus on the promise and know He has prepared the place for us to be with Him forever!

Are you sure of your salvation? If so, praise Him for the promise to come! If not, pray that you will confess your transgressions with your mouth and believe in your heart that Jesus is your Lord and Savior. He wants you to have a place in His mansion with many rooms. He wants to put your name in His book and give you all that is waiting for you. He will come again to take you to Himself if you believe.

He wants all to have eternal life and is waiting for you to tell them about His promises before they pass from this earth. What are you waiting for?

# December 16

*"Let what you say be simply 'Yes' or 'No'; anything more than this comes from evil."*
*Matthew 5:37*

Jesus wants us to commit to Him without wavering. He wants our Yes to be Yes and our No to be No. He does not want us second-guessing or questioning everything He puts in our hearts. The world will try to convince us we might offend someone by our proclamation of faith. There are times we tend to shrink back and change our minds about what Jesus tells us to share because we are listening to the culture and not to Jesus. Anything that is not from Jesus can be from evil.

You will recognize His voice when you stay focused on Jesus through your prayers and reading His Word. He speaks to you when you set your heart and mind on Him and His will. He speaks truth and never leads you astray. Listen only to Jesus!

Aim to stay close to Jesus focused on Jesus in all you do so the world will not lead you down the wrong path. If you spend more time with Jesus, He will show you the way to live. Stay close to Jesus and He will be your GPS to keep you on the right track with His power and protection.

HE SPEAKS TO ME

# December 17

*"This was the Lord's doing, and it is marvelous in our eyes?"*
*Mark 12:11*

God can turn things around and do great things with what was meant for harm. He does what He pleases. He brings life to death and blessings to curses. He will brighten a path with His light even in the darkest times. Understand that God in His mercy can turn things around. His marvelous plans are reminders of how His mercy runs deep and wide.

What problem are you facing right now? You can find your way out if you choose to go the extra mile with God by your side. He sees how much you are struggling and will overshadow you with His grace upon grace when you call upon Him. There is nothing too great for Him to work out.

Pray to let go of whatever is troubling you so you can be released from any stress that continues to overwhelm you. You are too blessed to be so stressed. Remember the day you made Him your Lord and believe He will replace your stress with His peace!

# December 18

*"This is the work of God, that you believe in him whom he has sent."*
**John 6:29**

Jesus answered the crowd's question about what they needed to be doing to do the works that God requires. He said the most important aspect to doing His work is to believe in Him. He wants us to discard doubt so belief will rise to the surface. Since sin has separated us from Him, God brought saving grace in the person of Jesus Christ so we would believe and have a relationship with God. Adam's one sin brought condemnation for everyone, but Christ's one act of righteousness brought a right relationship with God.

Do you believe in the Son of God? He came to set you free and have a relationship with you. He wants you to ask for forgiveness so you can walk in freedom. Settle in your heart to live connected to Jesus so sin will not have power over you.

Where are you? God asks this question because He wants you to make your home with Him. You cannot hide from God who is mighty and powerful over all. Answer Him when He calls you and come to your faithful Father.

HE SPEAKS TO ME

# *December 19*

*"No one can come to me unless the Father who sent me draws him. And I will raise him up on the last day."*
**John 6:44**

Jesus reminds us that no one can come to Jesus unless the Father brings us to Him. The Father will draw us to Himself as we seek Him. He will answer us as we call upon Him and tell Him we need a Savior. Then He will bring Jesus to us when we confess that we are sinners in need of a Savior and set our heart to believe in Jesus.

You were once a sinner walking dead in your trespasses following the world and the passions of your flesh. But God being rich in mercy, because of His great love for you, made you alive together with Christ. It is by grace you have been saved through faith. It is the gift of God not as a result of your works, but your faith.

What a joy we have in Jesus Christ! Not only do we have Jesus to save us from our sins right now, but we have a Savior who will raise us up with Him on the last day to live with Him forever and ever. Open your gift from God and believe you are worthy to receive it!

# December 20

*"Do you now believe?"*
**John 16:31**

J esus asks us this very critical and powerful question for us to ponder. He wanted all to see Him as Lord and ask Him into our hearts. He prayed the people who saw Him would set aside all doubt and see He was truly the Son of God sent for us. He wanted His followers to remain faithful and feel His peace when the pain and persecution comes. We will all be held accountable before God for all we have done and said so it is imperative we repent and believe today!

Open your heart to believe and walk by faith. Jesus is calling you to set aside doubt, worry, and fear. He gives peace that the world cannot give to you. Peace will make its home in you so you will never feel alone. Bring it all to the foot of the cross where Jesus is waiting for you with open arms.

What are you waiting for? He can take away the burdens you are carrying. Oh, how marvelous is your Savior's love for you that He carried your sins when He carried the cross to calvary and died to give you freedom from those sins!

# December 21

*"See my hands and my feet, that it is I myself.*
*Touch me, and see. For a spirit does not have flesh*
*and bones as you see that I have."*
*Luke 24:39*

Jesus came back to show His disciples He had defeated death and rose again to new life as He had said. Some who saw Him believed, but others did not. He showed them His hands and feet where the nails had penetrated His flesh and bones. They touched Him to see it was truly the Son of Man, Jesus Christ, in their midst. They believed because they saw the proof of His death in the flesh. But, blessed are those who believe without seeing and walk by faith and not by sight!

Are you walking by faith or by sight? Jesus wants to see you remaining faithful so others will see and want to know Jesus as Lord. When faith rises, fear disappears. People who do not know Jesus will see their need for the saving grace He brings because of the love you give them.

Who will you tell about the love of Jesus? He came to give His love and set everyone free! Stand firm and be a light wherever your feet are planted. He needs you!

# December 22

*"Nevertheless, I tell you the truth: it is to your advantage that I go away, for if I do not go away, the Helper will not come to you. But if I go, I will send him to you."*
*John 16:7*

Jesus told His disciples He would send the Helper, the Holy Spirit, to be with them forever. He reminded them that it was to their advantage that He went away so the Holy Spirit would come to them. They did not fully understand when Jesus spoke these words, but they knew Jesus would do what He had promised. Knowing He would be leaving them was difficult, but believing His Spirit would be come to them and be with them forever was comforting.

Jesus gives you the promised Holy Spirit when you believe. He will teach you and help you when you need guidance. Cling to the Spirit of truth so He can show you the way. He is your ever-present help in trouble and your source of light and discernment.

Lay aside every weight and cling to the Spirit inside of you who will guide you to all truth. Listen and be encouraged for your Lord has empowered you with life!

# December 23

*"I am the true vine,
and my Father is the vinedresser."*
**John 15:1**

Jesus shared this to His disciples right before He was betrayed by Judas. He wanted His disciples to hear how they were to live a fruitful life. We can also live a life close to the vine if we abide in Jesus. He stated He is the true vine who would sustain all and give life. The Father is our vinedresser who helps us grow. The Spirit is the life source who gives life to the vine so it will bear fruit. The Father, Son, and the Holy Spirit work together as one in our lives so we can receive life-giving power to produce good fruit.

Bearing fruit in your life will be the result of a close and intimate relationship with Jesus Christ. You will produce a fruitful, spiritual life where His sap flows. He will bless you richly with His amazing sap that never stops nourishing the branches. Will you remain in Jesus so He can infuse you with His Spirit?

Jesus gives you the Spirit to enrich with His love and the Word to enlighten you with His truth. When you are walking with the Spirit and the Word, you will be actively living how Jesus wants you to live.

# December 24

*"He will glorify me, for he will take what is mine*
*and declare it to you."*
**John 16:14**

Jesus wanted us to know the Holy Spirit glorifies Him. When we make Jesus our Lord, the Holy Spirit will make His home in us. The Spirit's presence in us allows us to magnify and worship Jesus. When we ask Jesus to live in us and we walk in the power of the Spirit, we will have the same glory revealed to us. The Spirit declares all that is ours when we are living close to Him.

Are you living close to Jesus and choosing to have His Spirit as power living in you? He manifests Himself to all who obey Him and walk in the truth of the Word and the power of the Spirit. You can overcome everything you are struggling with when you surrender all and let Jesus breathe His life-giving powerful Spirit on you.

Feel the presence of Jesus over you. Hear His voice comforting you. With Jesus in your heart and the Spirit in your soul, you will fully experience the power and love of the Savior who was born to give you new life. Celebrate His love for you and praise Him for showing you His glory!

# December 25

*"Until now you have asked nothing in my name.*
*Ask, and you will receive, that your joy may be full."*
*John 16:24*

Full joy is ours in Christ! Without Christ living in us, we cannot know the joy He promises. He even tells us we can ask anything in His name, and we shall receive according to His will so our joy would be full. Maybe we are not receiving because we are not asking with the right motive or with faith to overcome all. Or we ask for His will to be done, but we forget to ask in the name of Jesus so He will be glorified. When our hearts are close to Him, we can ask, and He will give us the desires of our hearts.

What are the desires of your heart? Delight yourself in the Lord and He will show you what His desires are for you. The closer you get to Him, the more His desires will be in sync with yours.

What areas of your heart are still not full of the joy of Jesus? Seek His will for you and ask Him to show you where you need to come closer to Him. When you humble yourself before Him, He fills you up with more of Him. His plan is that you will be faithful so He can conquer any doubt and wipe away any fear.

# December 26

*"Let not your hearts be troubled.*
*Believe in God; believe also in me."*
*John 14:1*

Jesus told us to not let our hearts be troubled. He wanted us to believe in God and believe also in Him. He knew there would be things that would happen in our lives we would not understand, but he wanted us to take heart because He had overcome the world for us. He knew life would bring us challenges, but He also knew He would fight for us so nothing could separate us from the love of God.

Are you having trouble seeing the way out of the pain that brings you down? Keep your eyes focused on Jesus and He will show you the way out. He promises to give you all you need to fight the good fight of the faith. Only Jesus can give you courage to win the battle.

Are you prepared to face your giants? Bring Jesus to the fight and you will be victorious. He knows what you will be facing and how He can help you conquer these giants. He will infuse you with power and strength. Just trust Him for all you need and let Him pour wisdom and grace upon you so you can live in victory again and again!

HE SPEAKS TO ME

# December 27

*"Truly, truly, I say to you, whoever believes in me will also do the works that I do; and greater works than these will he do, because I am going to the Father."*
*John 14:12*

If we believe in Jesus, He will allow us to do the works He is doing and greater works for the Lord. He wants us to seek Him for what He wants to do through us. Only Jesus can infuse us with the will and the desire to work for Him in greater ways. He has many plans for us and will show us exactly what those are when we trust Him with all our hearts and lean not on our own understanding.

What do you believe the greater works are that Jesus wants you to do? He has set you aside to give you these new opportunities to work for His kingdom. He wants you and will wait for your willing heart and giving hands and feet. He has set you aside for His purposes. Do not worry but wait for the instructions and then get to work.

Anticipate His promptings and work effectively to bring His love to life. You will not regret the time you have spent getting to know your Lord.

# December 28

*"Take heart; it is I. Do not be afraid."*
*Matthew 14:27*

Jesus sees us and wants us to see Him. He asks us to take heart because He is with us. When we take our eyes off our problems and give Jesus our full attention, He will produce new hope in us. Only Jesus can take what was troubling us and make us whole again. We are made new in Christ when we set our minds on Him and not our fears. Stop fearing and start trusting!

He has set you apart for His glory and given you the determination to finish your race faithfully. Will you come to His throne of grace and stop turning toward those who are bringing you down and causing you to stumble? They do not have your best interests at heart but are wishing you would fall.

But Jesus, full of grace, will bring you the truth and show you how you can rise above it all. He sees those who are trying to hurt you. He loves you so much that He will give you the courage to finish strong and the faith to fight. Be strong and courageous and do not fear them because your Lord is near to you. He will surely do something new in you with the faith He has planted in your heart.

# December 29

*"You did not choose me, but I chose you and appointed you that you should go and bear fruit and that your fruit should abide, so that whatever you ask the Father in my name, he may give it to you."*
**John 15:16**

Jesus chose us to go and bear fruit so that our fruit may abide in Him. The Father gave us the gift of salvation through Jesus so we could abide in Him. When we make Jesus our Lord, He will begin the change in us from the inside out. As a result of this change, we will have joy that remains forever!

He has appointed you to certain people and opportunities that are hand-picked just for you. He knows how you can make a difference by bearing fruit where He plants your feet. Your ministry can start right where you live and work. Think of all the people you encounter regularly. Do they know you love and follow Jesus? If so, you are bearing fruit, and if not, make every effort to let your light shine so they can know Jesus, too.

Start praying for opportunities for the Holy Spirit to give you words to share with people. He will help you if you ask the Father in the name of Jesus. Be a fruit-bearer for Jesus!

# December 30

*"Whoever has my commandments and keeps them,*
*he it is who loves me. And he who loves me will be*
*loved by my Father, and I will love him and*
*manifest myself to him."*
**John 14:21**

Jesus taught us to obey the commandments given by the Father. When we do obey them and follow Jesus, we show our love for Jesus. These commands are not burdensome but are for our own good. He looks far and wide for those who are seeking Him with their whole hearts and putting Him before all else. He will reward us with His presence when we show our love for Him in our actions and our words.

The Father will manifest Himself to you when you choose to obey Him and love Him with all your heart. Your reward is a close relationship with Jesus and the Father.

Think of the last time you saw something so amazing that you knew it was a gift from the Father above made just for you. Remember the feeling you felt inside knowing that He wanted you to see this special revelation of His love. Look around and see what He is revealing to you faithful servant!

# December 31

*"If anyone loves me, he will keep my word, and my Father will love him, and we will come to him and make our home with him."*
**John 14:23**

We are created to love our Savior and worship Him. The Father made us in His image to know we are loved and to love Him with all our heart, soul, and mind. When we make the choice to love Him, He softens our heart with His compassion and empowers our soul with His Spirit. He wants all to make the choice to love so He can come to us and make His home within us.

Come home to Jesus. If you love Him, keep His word, and trust Him with all your heart. Your faith will give you confidence to know you were chosen by Jesus to go and make disciples. He will bless you with courage to do things that once seemed impossible. Your hands and feet will go to places and serve in areas where you never thought you would be.

There is no greater love than this than to lay down one's life for one's friends. Praise Jesus today that He did this for you!. He loved you so much that He went to the cross for you so you could be with Him forever!

# The Greatest Gift

You have been given the greatest gift from the loving Father
above, Jesus Christ, His Son, to cherish and to love!

His living water is for you and for me,
Drink it now so that you can be free!

Take your cup and let Jesus fill the holes,
He is the only one who will comfort your soul!

He knows what you are facing, and He knows how you feel,
Give Him your heart so that you can be healed!

The time is now and the hour of His return is coming,
Say yes to Jesus and stop your running!

He wants to have a relationship with you,
So do not wait any longer, not even a minute or two!

He is right beside you patiently waiting once more,
For your heart to be touched and your spirit to soar!

Open your gift and stand firm with Jesus Christ,
And you will have joy the rest of your life!

*"Jesus answered her, 'If you knew the gift of God and who it is
that asks you for a drink, you would have asked him and he
would have given you living water.'"*
*John 4:10*

*"But whoever drinks of the water that I will give him will never
be thirsty again. The water that I will give him will become in
him a spring of water welling up to eternal life."*
*John 4:14*

Written by Jill Lowry
Jilllowryministries.com

HE SPEAKS TO ME
**377**

# Looking for More?

## A Year of Daily Devotionals for One-on-One Time with God

## Available on Amazon
https://www.amazon.com/dp/B08LTRBDN5

3 - Minute Devotionals to Revive Your Heart

## Available on Amazon
https://www.amazon.com/dp/B0C55RR4MY

# Prayers

## FROM THE

# HEART

God-Size Your Prayers to Find Your Destiny

## Available on Amazon

https://www.amazon.com/dp/B07TW7YMHV

# Also By Jill Lowry

A Year of Daily Devotionals to
Ignite Your Heart for Jesus

## Available on Amazon
https://www.amazon.com/dp/B07HKK2MN9

# A YEAR OF WEEKLY DEVOTIONALS

# FINDING
# JOY
## in Jesus

## Available on Amazon

# Promises
## OF
# HOPE

## Available on Amazon
https://www.amazon.com/dp/B079VTNMY9

## Available Here:
https://www.amazon.com/dp/B093XY7HPZ

# Prayer Journals also Available on Amazon

https://www.amazon.com/dp/1693027763

https://www.amazon.com/dp/0578633906

# ABOUT THE AUTHOR

Jill Lowry is an ardent follower of Jesus who has a desire and passion to communicate His truth. Inspired by the Holy Spirit, her writings combine the accuracy of a scholar with the practicality of a wife and mother. Jill grew up in San Antonio, Texas. She graduated from the University of Texas with a Bachelor of Business Administration in Marketing and holds a law degree from St. Mary's University School of Law.

Jill is the founder and president of a student mentoring and food program, Mt Vernon Cares, created for at-risk students at the local High School. She is on the Women's Ministry Leadership Team for the Heart to Heart women's ministry at First Baptist Church Mt.Vernon. Her heart is that women of all ages would grow their relationship with Jesus. Jill is the host of a faith-based weekly radio talk show and podcast, Real Life Real People Radio. She also co-hosts another podcast, Journey with Jesus, where two friends share truths and positivity about how to find joy in Jesus. In addition, Jill is a contributing partner on Bible.com where you can read more of her devotionals.

Jill takes every opportunity to pray with friends and neighbors in need and considers intercessory prayer a vital part of her ministry. She is part of a women's prayer warrior team that meets each week to pray for those in need of prayer.

Visit her website for more information on these ministries and subscribe to receive inspirational daily prayers. http://www.jilllowryministries.com

Made in United States
Orlando, FL
15 December 2024

55789268R00222